The Economy of the
Kingdom of God

The Economy of the Kingdom of God

SOON PAIK

Foreword by Eung Yul Ryu

RESOURCE *Publications* • Eugene, Oregon

THE ECONOMY OF THE KINGDOM OF GOD

Copyright © 2022 Soon Paik. All rights reserved. Except for brief quotations in critical publications or reviews, no part of this book may be reproduced in any manner without prior written permission from the publisher. Write: Permissions, Wipf and Stock Publishers, 199 W. 8th Ave., Suite 3, Eugene, OR 97401.

Resource Publications
An Imprint of Wipf and Stock Publishers
199 W. 8th Ave., Suite 3
Eugene, OR 97401

www.wipfandstock.com

PAPERBACK ISBN: 978-1-6667-4961-8
HARDCOVER ISBN: 978-1-6667-4962-5
EBOOK ISBN: 978-1-6667-4963-2

12/08/22

Scripture quotations marked (NIV) are taken from the Holy Bible, New International Version®, NIV®. Copyright © 1973, 1978, 1984 by Biblica, Inc.™ Used by permission of Zondervan. All rights reserved worldwide.

Contents

Foreword by Eung Yul Ryu | vii

Introduction | ix

Chapter 1: The Life of the Kingdom of God | 1

Chapter 2: Economic Men and Women and "Good and Faithful Servant" (Matt 25:21) | 8

Chapter 3: Economic Decision-Making and "You Shall Not Steal" (Exod 20:15) | 14

Chapter 4: Economic Trade (Exchange) and "There Are Different Kinds of Gifts" (1 Cor 12:4) | 18

Chapter 5: National Economy and "Every Good Tree Bears Good Fruit" (Matt 7:17) | 24

Chapter 6: Production of Labor and "Fill the Earth and Subdue It" (Gen 1:28) | 29

Chapter 7: Production of Capital and "Your Young Men Will See Visions" (Joel 2:28) | 37

Chapter 8: Production Optimization and "He Sold All He Had and Bought That Field" (Matt 13:44) | 44

Chapter 9: Consumption of Freedom and "You Are Free to Eat" (Gen 2:16) | 49

Chapter 10: Consumption of Temptation and "You Must Not Eat from the Tree of the Knowledge of Good and Evil" (Gen 2:17) | 52

Contents

Chapter 11: Economy of the Family and "They Will Become One Flesh" (Gen 2:24) | 57

Chapter 12: Social Welfare Function and "Be Holy, Because I Am Holy" (Lev 11:45) | 64

Chapter 13: Economic Policies and "The Noble Man Makes Noble Plans" (Isa 32:8) | 69

Chapter 14: The Kingdom of God in the Bible: The Glorious Biblical Life | 74

Chapter 15: Conclusion | 89

Bibliography | 93

Foreword

I AM VERY APPRECIATIVE of and excited to read *The Economy of the Kingdom of God*, written by Dr. Soon Paik, a faithful elder and a noted economist, because this book could be read as an excellent reference but not be written by just anybody. Dr. Paik analyzes economic activities by the vision of the Bible, in detail, like latitudes and longitudes. This book contains both the faith of a respectable elder and the intelligent knowledge of a knowledgeable economist.

Economics is hard to understand, even for intellectuals, while economic living is a whole area of life even for children. Economic activities are to be handled as an essential area of the kingdom of God; however, they should not hold all power, seizing the position of God.

In this book, economic concepts are to be reevaluated from the point of view of the kingdom of God, and then the book proposes biblical economic perspectives as people in the kingdom of God. This book is to be a stepping stone for the living of believers that so pleases God, as everyone learns the biblical economic view at its core.

Rev. Eung Yul Ryu
senior pastor of Korean Central Presbyterian Church of Washington

Introduction

I BECAME A CHRISTIAN at seventeen years old when my friend introduced me as a junior high school student to the Gospel Church located in the fifth Jongro, Seoul, Republic of Korea where I listened to the sermons by senior pastor Rev. Dong Shik Jee, attended the Bible studies, and accepted Jesus Christ as Lord.

At that time, I had read many philosophy books in order to search for my identity and the righteousness of human beings. What is absolute righteousness? By listening to Rev. Dong Shik Jee's sermons and reading the Bible, I recognized that all human beings are sinners, and the ruler of absolute righteousness is God, to whom the way is Jesus Christ. While serving in the ROK Air Force for four years after the April 19, 1960, demonstration in my junior year and the May 16, 1961, military coup d'ê'tat in my senior year, I recognized the poverty of the ROK and understood the five-year economic development plan by the government. After military service for four years, I decided to study economics rather than a lawyer's career and then went to the United States to study economics in 1968.

I got a master's degree in economics from The Ohio University and a PhD in economics from West Virginia University, and have served the US Department of Labor for thirty years, retiring as a senior economist in 2015. Now, I am teaching economics at Washington University of Virginia. And I have served the Korean Central Presbyterian Church of Washington, Centreville, Virginia, as a senior elder. As I have lived as a Christian and at the same time as an economist for more than a half century in the United States, I

Introduction

have tried very hard to combine biblical truths and economic theories in terms of the life of the kingdom of God.

The life of the kingdom of God coming near (Matt 3:17—present aspect of the kingdom of God) has two kinds of the life: one is the life entering the rule of God in terms of his natural character (the spiritual life), and the other is the life living the rule of God in terms of his active or moral character (the glorious life). And the glorious life has two kinds: one is the glorious economic life living economic activities, and the other is the glorious biblical life living the parables explained by Jesus Christ in the four Gospels.

This book will be helpful to develop Christian life as the life of the kingdom of God coming near under the present world, progressing toward postmodernism and diversity in its value system.

It is a book describing my confession of the Christian faith to be delivered to God. I give special thanks to Rev. Eung Yul Ryu who wrote the recommendation for me and to the editors.

I deliver this book to my wife, Kyung Mi Ahn, who has prayed for me at all times; and to my son, Hyun Paik; my daughter-in-law, Soo Hyun Kim; and my grandsons, San Paik and Dou Paik.

Soon Paik
Reston, Virginia, United States

CHAPTER 1

The Life of the Kingdom of God

THE CHRISTIAN FAITH IS to live in the kingdom of God ("being sure of what we hope for and certain of what we do not see" [Heb 11:1]).

Nelson's Illustrated Bible Dictionary defines the kingdom of God (kingdom of heaven) as the country ruled by the grace of God.[1] However, there are two aspects of the kingdom of God as depicted in the Bible:

> One is the present aspect;
>
> another is the future aspect.

The future aspect of the kingdom of God is the kingdom where God completes in ruling by grace, which is depicted in the Bible as the garden of Eden, the one indicated in the advent of Christ, and a new heaven and a new earth in Revelation.

> Now the Lord God had planted a garden in the east, in Eden, and there he put the man he had formed. (Gen 2:8)

A garden in Eden is the only place where happiness, peace, and pleasure are filled with fullness, and about which all the prophets in the Old Testament prophesied.

---

1. Lockyer, *Nelson's Illustrated Bible Dictionary*, 617.

> And if I go and prepare a place for you, I will come back and take you to be with me that you also may be where I am. (John 14:3)

Someday in the second advent of Christ, Jesus takes us to the place, the kingdom of God with glory.

> Then I saw a new heaven and a new earth, for the first heaven and the first earth passed away, and there was no longer any sea. (Rev 21:1)

A new heaven and a new earth without a sea is the future aspect of the kingdom of God.

While the future aspect of the kingdom of God depicted by the Bible in a garden of Eden, in the second advent of Christ, and in a new heaven and a new earth is the perfect kingdom of God with completion, the present aspect of the kingdom of God purposes for Jesus to teach us and lead us to the way toward the future aspect of the completed kingdom of God. Let us illustrate what is the present aspect of the kingdom of God from Jesus's teachings in the four Gospels.

The purpose of Jesus's coming in this world is to teach the present aspect of the kingdom of God and to lead to the way of living as the people of the kingdom of God. After Jesus was baptized by John and tested by Satan in the wildness and prayed without food for forty days, he proclaimed:

> Repent, for the kingdom of heaven has come near. (Matt 4:17)

What country is the kingdom of God that has come near and where we live? What is the life of the present aspect of the kingdom of God? These are what he taught us.

The life of the present aspect of the kingdom of God is to live by submitting to and following and developing the rule by God as characterized by the identity of God. What is the rule by God? Even though the rule by God cannot be completely clarified, the attributes or the inherent characteristics of God depict the rule by God, which includes two kinds of the characteristics of God, namely, the natural characteristics and the actual or moral characteristics.

The Life of the Kingdom of God

The natural characteristics of God are:

1. God is Spiritual
2. God is Changeless
3. God is All-Powerful
4. God is All-Knowing
5. God is Omnipresent
6. God is Eternal

And the actual or moral characteristics of God are:

1. God is Glorious
2. God is Holy
3. God is Righteous
4. God is Gracious and Loving
5. God is Truthful
6. God is Wise

We, human beings, are the children of God. So, we have to live the present aspect of the kingdom of God by living God's rule characterized by the natural and actual or moral characteristics of God. The lives to live the rule of God by submitting to and following and developing God's characters are classified into two lives:

1. The spiritual life by living God's rule in terms of God's natural characteristics
2. The glorious life by living God's rule in terms of God's actual or moral characteristics

Jesus said to his disciples on his last Passover dinner:

> I am the vine; you are the branches. If you remain in me and I in you, you will bear much fruit; apart from me you can do nothing. (John 15:5)

The Christian cannot live the life by leaving Jesus; we as the branches of the vine, Jesus, should attach to the vine, Jesus, so that the Christian should bear much fruit. Christians as the branches of the vine should satisfy two elements for bearing much fruit:

> One element is for us to live in Jesus;

another element is for Jesus to live in us.

The first element for us to live in Jesus indicates the spiritual life, while the second element for Jesus to live in us explains the glorious life. And then we as the faithful Christian could bear much fruit as Jesus expects.

THE SPIRITUAL LIFE

Since God is spirit (John 4:24), the first present aspect required in the kingdom of God is to be in God (Jesus). The spiritual life implies living God's rule in terms of his natural characteristics, the life being indicated as three Ps: as the People of God, Father of creation and changeless; as the Pupils of Jesus Christ, who has all power and all knowledge; and as Persons of the Spirit, who is everywhere and eternal. The Bible teaches three truths concerning the spiritual life in the present aspect of the kingdom of God.

The First Biblical Truth on the Spiritual Life

Entering into the present aspect of the kingdom of God is to live as the people of God by submitting to his will and the objectives of his creation and by following and developing his characteristic of changelessness.

> But seek first his kingdom and his righteousness, and all these things will be given to you as well. (Matt 6:33)
>
> Not everyone who says to me, "Lord, Lord," will enter the kingdom of heaven, but only the one who does the will of my Father who is in heaven. (Matt 7:21)
>
> He has brought down rulers from their thrones but has lifted up the humble. (Luke 1:52)

The Life of the Kingdom of God

The Second Biblical Truth on the Spiritual Life

Entering into the present aspect of his kingdom is to live as the pupils of Jesus Christ by having faith in the gospel with all power and all knowledge, to follow Jesus Christ with the cross given to him, and to deliver Jesus's teachings.

> Then Jesus said to his disciples, "If anyone would come after me, he must deny himself and take up his cross and follow me. (Matt 16:24)
>
> But whoever practices and teaches these commands will be called great in the kingdom of heaven. (Matt 5:19)
>
> As you go, proclaim this message: "The kingdom of heaven has come near." (Matt 10:7)

The Third Biblical Truth on the Spiritual Life

Entering into the present aspect of his kingdom is to live as persons of the Spirit who is everywhere and eternal, not only by submitting to the Spirit God but also following and developing his guidance, with the vision given by the Spirit, with the gifts of the Spirit and with the fruit of the Spirit, as a Spirit-fulfilment Christian.

> And afterward, I will pour out my Spirit on all people. Your sons and daughters will prophesy, your old men will dream dreams, your young men will see visions. (Joel 2:28)
>
> There are different kinds of gifts, but the same Spirit. (1 Cor 12:4)
>
> But the fruit of the Spirit is love, joy, peace, patience, kindness, goodness, faithfulness, gentleness and self-control. Against such things there is no law. (Gal 5:22–23)
>
> Because the kingdom of God in your midst. (Luke 17:21)
>
> From that time on Jesus began to preach, "Repent, for the kingdom of heaven has come near." (Matt 4:17)
>
> Blessed are the poor in spirit, for theirs is the kingdom of heaven. (Matt 5:3)

> But if it is by the Spirit of God that I drive out demons, then the kingdom of God has come upon you. (Matt 12:28)
>
> Jesus answered, "Very truly I tell you, no one can enter the kingdom of God unless they are born of water and the Spirit. (John 3:5)
>
> As you go, proclaim this message: "The kingdom of heaven has come near." (Matt 10:7)

THE GLORIOUS LIFE IN THE KINGDOM OF GOD

The Bible teaches us to live the glorious life in the present aspect of his kingdom by living God's rule in terms of his actual or moral characteristics in this world, such as glory, holiness, righteousness, grace and love, truthfulness, and wisdom. The glorious life is to be indicated as the three Ps of life, including the Purpose, the Policies, and the Process of Life. The Purpose is God's glory; the Policies are God's holiness and righteousness; and the Processes are God's love, truth, and wisdom.

There are two contents in the glorious life in the present aspect of his kingdom. One content is the glorious life as taught in the parables by Jesus in his life on this earth, which will be illustrated in chapter 14, as the glorious biblical life.

The other content is the glorious life in the economic areas in which the human beings should experience daily life. Biblical truths can be studied and illustrated according to the main subjects of the glorious economic life in the economic areas that have been established in economic theory, namely:

1. The identity of economic men and women
2. Principles of economy
3. Production
4. Consumption
5. Distribution
6. Economic policies

The identity of men and women will be explored in chapter 2, principles of economy in chapters 3 to 5, production in chapters 6 to 8, consumption in chapters 9 to 11, distribution in chapter 12, and policies in chapter 13.

CHAPTER 2

Economic Men and Women and "Good and Faithful Servant"

(Matt 25:21)

The main economic concept of economics is the identity of the economic man and woman (who is the economic man or woman?).

Even if this world is infected fully with corruption, depravity, and darkness, we are to live the present aspect of his kingdom that Jesus proclaimed at the beginning of his preaching: "Repent, for the kingdom of heaven has come near" (Matt 4:17). Lives in the present aspect of his kingdom are of two kinds, namely, the spiritual life and the glorious life.

The spiritual life of the present aspect of the kingdom of God is the critical content of Christian faith; however, the glorious life itself includes the important content in which God's will and provision are to be clarified by developing and enhancing his glory.

The glorious economic life should include the economic elements that would occupy totally all the parts of our lives. The economic elements are to be explained as a flow model that contains two major economic agents, namely, the suppliers (producers) and the demanders (consumers). In the economic flow model, there are two markets, the product market and the production factors market. The product market is the market where the products (goods

Economic Men and Women and "Good and Faithful Servant"

and services) produced by the suppliers (producers) are to be sold and bought by the demanders (consumers). And the production factors market is the market where the producers are to buy the production factors (raw materials, labor, capital, etc.) to produce the goods and services, and the consumers are to supply the production factors.

In the economic flow model including two markets, the main players are the suppliers (producers) and the demanders (consumers): the economic man and woman. Here we have to ask the very significant question: who are the economic man and woman? What is the identity of the economic man and woman? What is their objective or their motive?

Two issues regarding the identity of economic man and woman are self-interest and rationality.

Economic theory is based on the identity of the economic man and woman, which is self-interest and rationalism. Adam Smith, called a father of economics, maintained in his famous book titled *The Wealth of Nations* (1776) that a big metropolitan city like Paris in France was operated very well by "invisible hands" as the citizens pursued their own self-interests and rational decisions.[1]

The self-interest to be pursued by Adam Smith has to be the "enlightened self-interest" that understands and allows the truth that other people also have their own self-interests. However, as enlightened self-interests have not been maintained, the animal spirits of pursuing only one's own interests are to be pursued the economic activities, which John Maynard Keynes, the famous economist in Britain, argued.[2]

We have experienced two major bubble economies, namely, the information technology bubble in the 1990s and the housing bubble in 2009, which happened due to irrational investment rushes in the New York stock exchange.

There has recently appeared a new economic analysis that has studied economic behaviors including animal spirits and irrational

---

1. Smith, *Wealth of Nations*, 7–11.
2. Keynes, *General Theory*, 3–24.

investments concerning the identity of the economic man and woman.

Here is the significant question concerning the biblical identity of the economic man and woman. Are there biblical self-interests and biblical rationality? What are biblical self-interests, if any? What is biblical rationality, if any?

THE FIRST BIBLICAL TRUTH ON SELF-INTEREST

The first biblical truth is the self-interest accompanying stewardship.

All economic behaviors are pursued by the attitude of self-interest with the purpose of implementing the stewardship given by God.

The Bible does not deny self-interest. There are two elements concerning the creation of mankind in God's own image (Gen 1:17). The first element of God's image is the autonomy to be implemented by his will and provisions, and the second element is the stewardship given to mankind to do God's truth, his righteousness, and his love. The image of God in the creation of mankind includes two elements of stewardship and of autonomy (self-interest).

The stewardship of "Love the Lord your God" (Deut 6:5) should be implemented with the attitude of self-interest such as "with all your heart and with all your soul and all your strength" (Deut 6:5). For the second commandment of "Love your neighbor as yourself" (Matt 22:5), the attitude of self-interest of "as yourself" is to be applied in order to do the stewardship of the second commandment of "love your neighbor."

Let us investigate the biblical self-interest accompanying the stewardship in Genesis chapters 1 through 3.

> God blessed them and said to them, "Be fruitful and increase in number: fill the earth and subdue it. Rule over the fish in the sea and the birds in the sky and over every living creature that moves on the ground." (Gen 1:28)

The stewardship assigned to mankind in creation is to "fill the earth," "subdue it," and "rule over." To perform the stewardship

Economic Men and Women and "Good and Faithful Servant"

assigned by God, mankind should pursue his assignment of the stewardship with the attitude of self-interest for enjoying the blessings "blessed" by God.

Since the post-twentieth century, the world has experienced decreasing population, retarding technology, and a deteriorating environment, which have resulted from the nonfulfillment of the stewardship to fill the earth, subdue it, and rule over it, without self-interest for the pleasure of the blessed.

> The Lord God took the man and put him in the Garden of Eden to work and take care of it. (Gen 2:15)

The stewardship assigned to man after God's creating the garden of Eden was to work and take care it. In order to implement successfully the assigned stewardship to work and take care of the garden, man withholds the attitude of self-interest for reward due to his faithfulness and sincerity.

The depravity of the world has constantly increased every day, especially since the start of the twenty-first century, for the stewardship to work and take care it has not been implemented without self-interest for the appreciation of reward toward the faithful mission.

> To the woman he said, "I will make your pains in childbearing very severe; with painful labor you will give birth to children. Your desire will be for your husband, and he will rule over you."
>
> To Adam he said, "Because you listened to your wife and ate fruit from the tree about which I commanded you, "You must not eat from it," cursed is the ground because of you: through painful toil you will eat food from it all the days of your life. (Gen 3:16–17)

The stewardship after the fall from the garden of Eden is to "give birth to children" and "your desire will be for your husband" for the woman, and to earn "food . . . all the days of your life" for man. The attitude of self-interest for woman is the "painful labor" of giving life to children, and that for man is the "painful toil" of working for food all his life.

The declining population and the separation of the family are due to the abandonment of woman's stewardship without her self-interest of painful labor, and the hungers of the world have resulted from the nonfulfillment of man's stewardship without his self-interest of painful toil.

THE SECOND BIBLICAL TRUTH ON RATIONALITY

The second biblical truth should be the rationality to be implemented together with the holiness and righteousness of God.

Rationality in our economic behaviors is based on theory and logic developed by our experiences, our knowledges, and our judgements. This rationality sometimes could result in the disaster of huge economic recessions such as the bubbles of information technology in 2000 and of housing in 2009.

Investments in the financial markets are surely the economic actions to induce national economic growth. However, as the investments increase tremendously due to the animal spirit desire by investors, especially in the financial markets, the phenomenon of price bubbling would result in the disaster of explosion for price falling, which could result in huge economic recessions.

Here, we need biblical rationality. The Bible provides the real rationality, which is based on God's absolute standards such as holiness (Lev 19:2) and perfection (Matt 5:48).

What are holiness and perfection as the standards of biblical rationality?

There are two contents:

The first content of biblical rationality is rational decisions by our individual purification founded upon the holiness of God and reverence for God.

> Let us purify ourselves from everything that contaminates body and spirit, perfecting holiness out of reverence for God. (2 Cor 7:1)

A good example of everything contaminating body and spirit is the animal spirit that pursues only his or her own self-interest for excessive profit and satisfaction by his or her economic behaviors without the consideration of others' self-interests. Purification means to keep and follow God's standards for economic principles, especially in investments.

The second content of biblical rationality is rational decisions based on the national worship of God's holiness and his righteousness.

> You alone are holy. All nations will come and worship before you, for your righteous acts have been revealed. (Rev 15:4)

Biblical rationality pursues not only rational decisions based on individual purification, but also those based on national worship for the holiness of God. Rational decision-making without individual purification and national worship for God's glory would result in severe economic recessions. Their good examples were the bubble-bursts of information technology bubbling in 2000 and of housing bubbling in 2009.

The biblical identity of the economic man and woman should be such that the economic man and woman have the enlightened self-interest accompanying the stewardship for the kingdom of God, and at the same time the rational decision-making with individual purification and national worship for the glory of God.

CHAPTER 3

Economic Decision-Making and "You Shall Not Steal"

(Exod 20:15)

THE ECONOMIC MAN AND woman are to be identified as those pursuing self-interest and rationality. For their economic behaviors, there are economic principles that have been established over the history of human beings and that they should keep and follow fairly.

There are three groups of economic principles: the first group is for the economic principles of economic decision-making, the second group is for the economic principles of the economic exchange, and the third group is for the economic principles of the economy as a whole.[1]

The economic principles of economic decision-making include the principles concerning trade-off, cost, marginality, and incentive.

The economic principles such as trade-off, cost, marginality, and incentive are related to private property rights. Once private property rights are to be allowed, the economic principles of decision-making are possible: doing the trade-off, calculating the cost, considering marginality, and following incentive.

---

1. Mankiw, *Principles of Economics*, 3–18, 65–92; Pindyck and Rubinfeld, *Microeconomics*, 19–58.

Economic Decision-Making and "You Shall Not Steal"

Concerning property rights, there are two significant questions to be asked for determining the economic systems that have been developed over last few centuries. Who owns the property rights? And who manages and operates the property rights?

The economic system of individual ownership and individual management of property rights is capitalism, while that of state ownership and state management is communism. Totalitarianism is the system of individual ownership and state management, and socialism is the system of state ownership and individual management. Capitalism, even with problems of income inequality, has produced tremendous economic growth over the world and times, for the system has been based upon private property rights.

Private property rights should be understood within the relationship of the aid programs to solve problems of the world poverty. Over the last century, especially since World War II, economic aid programs to the poor countries of Africa and Southeast Asia have been augmented by the advanced countries and international agencies such as the United Nations, the World Bank, and the IMF. These aid programs have helped decrease the world poverty problem to some degree, but they have not resulted in their expectations. For example, as the aid fund has been given to one village of the African country, the development programs of the aid fund could not succeed in their planned results, because that African village did not have the concept of private property right and at the same time any power of incentive for developing any economic behavior such as business, production, and investment.

Three economists named Abhijit Banerjee, Esther Duflo, and Michael Kremer, professors at MIT and Harvard University, were awarded the 2019 Nobel Prize in economics, for their experiments for the development of underdeveloped countries. Their experiments resulted in the requirement of investments to improve individual incentives for solving poverty by allowing private property rights, developing children through education, and improving public health, rather than direct investment in the programs themselves.[2]

---

2. Nobel Prize, "Press Release."

Individual ownership of the private property right means individual unlimited possession of the property right, and individual management of the private property right implies (1) individual unrestricted use, (2) individual unrestricted enjoyment, and (3) individual unrestricted disposal of the property right.

Here, the Christian has to ask the very significant question: Does the Bible allow private property right to the people of the kingdom of God? Through the Bible, there are three aspects concerning private property right.

THE FIRST BIBLICAL TRUTH ON PRIVATE PROPERTY RIGHT

The first biblical truth is that God owns absolute private property right by owning all the creatures and operating them according to his will and provision.

> In the beginning God created the heavens and the earth. (Gen 1:1)
>
> The earth is the Lord's and everything in it, the world, and all who live in it. (Ps 24:1)
>
> The heavens are yours, and yours also the earth; you founded the world and all that is in it. (Ps 89:11)
>
> For, "The earth is the Lord's and everything in it." (1 Cor 10:26)

THE SECOND BIBLICAL TRUTH ON PRIVATE PROPERTY RIGHT

The second biblical truth is that relative private property right is given to the human being in order to reveal God's absolute private property right.

> You shall not steal. (Exod 20:15)

This commandment indicates that the human being created in his own image is allowed relative individual unlimited possession.

Economic Decision-Making and "You Shall Not Steal"

You shall not covet your neighbor's house. (Exod 20:17)

This commandment implies that the human being in God's image has relative individual unlimited use, enjoyment, and disposal rights.

THE THIRD BIBLICAL TRUTH ON PRIVATE PROPERTY RIGHT

The third biblical truth is that the relative private property right is active and practical.

> But gives his food to the hungry and provides clothing for the naked. (Ezek 18:7)

The active and practical relative private property right indicates sharing one's own relative private property with others who do not hold their own relative private property rights.

Because the human being has the relative and practical private property right reflecting God's absolute private property right, the economic principles of trade-off, cost, marginality, and incentives can be efficiently and effectively applied for economic decision-making.

CHAPTER 4

Economic Trade (Exchange) and "There Are Different Kinds of Gifts"

(1 Cor 12:4)

THE NEXT ECONOMIC PRINCIPLES are the principles of economic exchange (trade).

In an addition to economic decision-making, economic exchange (trade) is a very important field of economic behaviors. There are three economic principles being applied to economic exchange, namely, the principles of the division of labor, competition, and the public sector.

The first issue of economic exchange is division of labor.

Adam Smith explained the principle of division of labor by using the example of pin usage in his famous book titled *The Wealth of Nations*. Getting the pin for sewing and making clothes needs all the processes of making the pin such as mining iron rocks, processing iron ore, cutting the iron ore into pins, supplying the pins to the market, and buying the pins for their usage in the market. All these steps and processes take a long time and require tremendous labor to get a pin for its usage. However, as all the processes of getting a pin to the final step are to be implemented for dividing the labor by different laborers and then are to be allowed for trade (exchange) among the different processes, getting a pin becomes easy, cheap,

Economic Trade (Exchange) and "There Are Different Kinds of Gifts"

and convenient. At the same time, the production and consumption of pins increase in huge amounts.

As shown in the example of pin usage, all economies can be increased tremendously in their scopes due to the trade on the basis of the principle of division of labor.

Is the principle of division of labor to be found in the Bible?

The Bible teaches the principle of division of labor with the principle of the division of gifts, services, and workings.

> There are different kinds of gifts, but the same Spirit.
> There are different kinds of service, but the same Lord.
> There are different kinds of working, but the same God works all of them in all men. (1 Cor 12:4–6)

Let us search for the biblical truth concerning the principle of the division of labor, which makes the living life of God's kingdom be prosperous, abundant, and wealthy.

THE FIRST BIBLICAL TRUTH ON THE DIVISION OF LABOR

The first biblical truth is that the division of labor (gifts, services, and workings) is to be assigned to different persons with the same one objective (one Spirit, one Lord, and one God).

The different kinds of gifts (abilities), of services (professions), and of workings (implements) have to be operated with one objective (management) in order to achieve growth, prosperity, and strength.

THE SECOND BIBLICAL TRUTH ON THE DIVISION OF LABOR

The second biblical truth is that the divisions of labor (gifts, services, and workings) have to work together as members of collaboration for life and living.

> The body is a unit, though it is made up of many parts; and though all its parts are many, they form one body. So it is with Christ. (1 Cor 12:12)
>
> Now you are the body of Christ, and each one of you is a part of it. (1 Cor 12:27)
>
> If one part suffers, every part suffers with it; if one part is honored, every part rejoices with it. (1 Cor 12:26)

The Christian as a member of the people of God's Kingdom should share the toils and honors that are resulted by any member's activity.

THE THIRD BIBLICAL TRUTH ON THE DIVISION OF LABOR

The third biblical truth is that the division of labor (gifts, services, and workings) should be implemented with the best means (ways).

> But eagerly desire the greater gifts. And now I will show you the most excellent way. (1 Cor 12:31)
>
> If I give all I possess to the poor and surrender my body to the flames, but have not love, I gain nothing. (1 Cor 13:3).
>
> Love is patient, love is kind, it does not envy, it does not boast, it is not proud. (1 Cor 13:4–7)
>
> But the fruit of the Spirit is love, joy, peace, patience, kindness, goodness, faithfulness, gentleness and self-control. (Gal 5:22–23)

As the division of labor (gifts, services, and workings) is implemented with the most excellent way indicated in the Bible (love of fifteen kinds indicated in 1 Cor 13:4–7; love of eight kinds indicated in Gal 5:22–23), the kingdom of God would grow and be prosperous with the expansion of his glory.

The second issue of economic exchange is competition.

In both the markets of production outputs and production factors, the second principle of competition is required to be applied for prosperous and active economic exchanges and trades.

Economic Trade (Exchange) and "There Are Different Kinds of Gifts"

Adam Smith argued that Paris was at that time the prosperous capital city of France by the invisible hand even without any management control by the government. That invisible hand means that each citizen of Paris pursued their own enlightened self-interest together with competition.

Joseph Schumpeter as a famous economist in the twentieth century has argued in his famous book titled *Capitalism, Socialism, and Democracy* that one of the main forces for the economy under the system of the capitalism is entrepreneurship in the market. The entrepreneur is to do business with his own idea in the competitive market.[1]

The Bible teaches three truths on competition and contest in the living life of God's kingdom.

THE FIRST BIBLICAL TRUTH ON COMPETITION

The first biblical truth is that the competitor or contestant should train hard and moderate temperament in order to win the game.

> Everyone who competes in the games goes into strict training. (1 Cor 9:25)

THE SECOND BIBLICAL TRUTH ON COMPETITION

The second biblical truth is that the competitor or the contestant should keep the laws and rules of the games to win the games.

> Similarly, if anyone competes as an athlete, he does not receive the victor's crown unless he competes according to the rules. (2 Tim 2:5)

The rules of the games should be based upon God's righteousness.

---

1. Schumpeter, *Capitalism, Socialism, and Democracy*, 59–86.

THE THIRD BIBLICAL TRUTH ON COMPETITION

The third biblical truth is that the competitor or the contestant with strict training and rule-keeping is guaranteed the crown of victory.

> I have fought the good fight, I have finished the race, I have kept the faith. Now there is in store for me the crown of righteousness, which the Lord, the righteous Judge, will award to ne on that day—and not only to me, but also to all who have longed for his appearing. (2 Tim 4:7–8)

> Blessed is the man who perseveres under trial, because when he has stood the test, he will receive the crown of life that God has promised to those who love him. (Jas 1:12)

> But being examples to the flock. And when the Chief Shepherd appears, you will receive the crown of glory that will never fade away. (1 Pet 5:3–4)

The third issue of economic exchange is the public sector.

The market as the main place of economic exchange and trade is not perfect and shows many negative consequences even though it generates economic growth and prosperity. These phenomena are called market failures, which include two features, namely, negative market externalities and market power.

The corporations as the producers in the market produce not only the goods and services for sale in the market, but also materials external to the market such as polluted waters and air, which are defined as negative market externalities.

At the same time, it happens that the product in the market is produced by only one supplier (monopoly) or a few suppliers (oligopoly). Market power generally results in a small amount of the product with a high price for monopoly or oligopoly profit.

Market failure of negative market externalities and market power cannot be solved by the market itself, and then it has to be solved and treated to the proper level by the public sector as the third agent.

Economic Trade (Exchange) and "There Are Different Kinds of Gifts"

There are two biblical truths on the principle of the public sector.

THE FIRST BIBLICAL TRUTH ON THE PUBLIC SECTOR

The first biblical truth is that market failure cannot be kept out of happenings, because economic man and woman are not perfect with sin's nature.

> Ah, sinful nation, a people loaded with guilt, a brood of evildoers, children given to corruption. (Isa 1:4)

THE SECOND BIBLICAL TRUTH ON THE PUBLIC SECTOR

The second biblical truth is that market failure should be corrected by the public sector according to God's law of righteousness.

> For the Lord is good and his love endures forever; his faithfulness continues through all generations. (Ps 100:5)
>
> Every good and perfect gift is from above, coming down from the Father of the heavenly lights, who does not change like shifting shadows. (Jas 1:17)
>
> Then you will be able to test and approve what God's will is—his good, pleasing and perfect will. (Rom 12:2)

As the principles of division of labor, competition, and the public sector are to be implemented according to the truths taught in the Bible, economic exchange and trade would be operated actively and then make the living life of the kingdom of God prosperous and wealthy.

CHAPTER 5

National Economy and "Every Good Tree Bears Good Fruit"

(Matt 7:17)

THE LAST ECONOMIC PRINCIPLE is the principle of the national economy as a whole.

The economic life has three concepts of economic decision-making, economic trade, and the national economy. Each area has its own economic principles to be applied for increasing and improving the efficiency and effectiveness of the economic operation.

The third concept, the national economy, includes the principles of the growth of the Gross Domestic Product (GDP), the moderation of inflation, and the increase of employment.

The first issue of the national economy is the growth of the GDP.

The scope of a national economy is indicated by the GDP, which measures the market values of total final goods and services produced within a year by the nation.

According to 2018 statistics, the world's GDP was about $80 trillion, of which the United States produced $21.3 trillion in the ranking of first, while China, Japan, and Germany produced $13.6 trillion, $5.3 trillion, and $4.2 trillion, respectively, in the rankings

National Economy and "Every Good Tree Bears Good Fruit"

of second, third, and fourth. South Korea's GDP was $1.5 trillion in the ranking of twelfth.[1]

There are two biblical truths concerning the principle of the growth of the GDP.

THE FIRST BIBLICAL TRUTH ON THE GDP

The first biblical truth is that the foundation and the structure of the GDP should be built and formulated systematically and strongly.

The four major components of the GDP are consumption, investment, government expenditure, and net export (total export minus total import). The growth of the GDP is to be dependent upon the growth of the four components of the GDP.

> Likewise every good tree bears good fruit. (Matt 7:17)

THE SECOND BIBLICAL TRUTH ON THE GDP

The second biblical truth is that the negative elements resulting in GDP recession should be removed from the GDP structure and components.

> He cuts off every branch in me that bears no fruit, while every branch that does bear fruit he prunes so that it will be even more fruitful. (John 15:2)

The U.S. GDP experienced two major recessions in the two decades beginning 2000 and 2008, which have been denoted as the dot-com bubble in 2000 and the housing bubble in 2008. These two bubbles happened due to the animal spirit for excessive investments for high capital gains in stocks and housing. The animal spirit is the branch that bears no fruit and should be pruned decisively.

The second issue of the national economy is the moderation of inflation (the economy of money).

Money x Velocity = Price x Real GDP (Nominal GDP)

---

1. See United States Bureau of Economic Analysis.

The important question on inflation (the price level in the national economy) concerns the relationship between inflation and the quantity of money. Do changes in the money supply affect the price level but not real variables (monetary neutrality)?

To answer this question, let introduce the quantity equation of money:

Money Quantity x Money Velocity = Price Level x Real GDP

Because the money velocity (circulation of money quantity over a year) is stable over time, changes in the quantity of money affect the price level and/or the real GDP. Most economists have agreed in their studies that changes in the money supply do not affect the real GDP and are related to price level (inflation) in the long run (over ten years—long-run monetary neutrality), while they affect the price level and the real GDP in the short run (short-run monetary non-neutrality).

For example, the U.S. money quantity equation in 2018 is:

M_2 x Velocity = Nominal GDP

$14.7 trillion x 1.45 = $21.3 trillion[2]

Either in the short run or the long run, the quantity of money is related to the price level (inflation).

As the principle of the moderation of inflation is related to the quantity of money as explained above, let's evaluate the biblical truths concerning money:

THE FIRST BIBLICAL TRUTH ON MONEY

The first biblical truth is that money should be used as a necessary tool but not be served as the master, and there is only one master to be served: God.

> No one can serve two masters. Either he will hate the one and love the other, or he will be devoted to the one and despise the other. You can serve both God and the other. You cannot serve both God and money. (Matt 6:24)

2. See United States Federal Reserve.

National Economy and "Every Good Tree Bears Good Fruit"

THE SECOND BIBLICAL TRUTH ON MONEY

The second biblical truth is that money should be earned not by dishonest means but by righteous ways.

> Dishonest money dwindles away, but he who gathers money little by little makes it grow. (Prov 13:11)

THE THIRD BIBLICAL TRUTH ON MONEY

The third biblical truth is that money should be spent for getting friendship.

To earn righteous human relationships is one of the best policies for the usage of money.

> I tell you, use worldly wealth to gain friends for yourselves, so that when it is gone, you will be welcomed into eternal dwellings. (Luke 16:9)

The third issue of the national economy is the increase of employment.

Employment is one of the significant indicators for the prosperous national economy. The national employment situation is indicated by unemployment statistics.

Since the coronavirus pandemic in 2020, the employment situations of the world showed disastrous phenomena in 2020, and in 2021 they improved in some degree. However, the unemployment statistics of the world still showed relatively very high in the later months of 2021.

The unemployment rates of the advanced economies of the U.S. and E.U. are 5.9% and 7.9%.[3]

Those of developing economies such as Brazil, Russia, India, and China are 14.7%, 4.9%, 9.2%, and 5.0%, according to the *Economist*.[4]

The biblical truths related to the principle of the increase of employment are:

3. United States BLS.
4. *Economist*, "Economic Data."

THE FIRST BIBLICAL TRUTH ON EMPLOYMENT

The first biblical truth is that employment should be for the lifetime of the living.

> Through painful toil you will eat of it all the days of your life. (Gen 3:17)

> By the sweat of your brow you will eat your food until your return to the ground. (Gen 3:19)

THE SECOND BIBLICAL TRUTH ON EMPLOYMENT

The second biblical truth is that rest should be exercised to increase the effectiveness of the labor.

> Six days do your work, but on the seventh day do not work, so that your ox and your donkey may rest and the slave born in your household, and the alien as well, may be refreshed. (Exod 23:12)

> Remember the Sabbath day by keeping it holy. Six days you shall labor and do all your work, but the seventh day is a Sabbath to the Lord your God. (Exod 20:8)

THE THIRD BIBLICAL TRUTH ON EMPLOYMENT

The third biblical truth is that the basic attitude of work is to do the work as serving God.

> Whatever you do, work at it with all your heart, as working for the Lord, not for men. (Col 3:23)

The growth of the GDP, the moderation of inflation, and the increase of employment imply the growth, moderation, and increase of the kingdom of God.

CHAPTER 6

Production of Labor and "Fill the Earth and Subdue It"

(Gen 1:28)

IN THE ECONOMY, THERE are two markets, namely, the products (goods and services) market and the production factors market. And the economy is comprised of three areas, including production (supply), consumption (demand), and distribution (sharing).

For production, two objectives are to be pursued: production expansion by production factor expansion, and production optimization of production factors and products. Production expansion includes production expansion by labor expansion and that by capital expansion, for labor and capital are two major production factors in production function (products are the function of labor and capital).

The first economic concept of production is the production expansion of labor.

Production expansion by labor is explained in this chapter, production expansion by capital in chapter 7, and production optimization in chapter 8.

The first issue of labor is population.

Labor should be understood in terms of three concepts, namely, population, labor force, and employment in economic theory.

The world population in 2019 was 7.7 billion and that of the U.S. 329 million.[1]

There have been two major problems concerning world population about which population scholars have argued:

The first population issue is that the world population growth is decreasing every year.

The birth rate per one thousand people was 22.5 in 2000 and decreased to 18.2 in 2019. The fertility rate per woman, which was 2.7 in 2000, fell to 2.2 in 2019; and for the U.S. it decreased from 2.00 in 2000 to 1.85 in 2019.

The second population issue is that the composition of the senior population over sixty-five years old has been increasing over the last decades.

The senior population composition rate was 7.0% in 2000 and increased to 9.5% in 2019. For the U.S. it increased from 13.0% in 2000 to 13.8% in 2019.

Peter Peterson, a famous population scholar, argued on the crisis of the increasing senior population in his best-selling book titled *Gray Dawn*. He predicted that in the middle and/or the later twenty-first century, the advanced countries in North America and the E.U., Japan, and Australia will be bankrupt, while the emerging and underdeveloped countries could occupy the world in terms of the population and of the economy. For the increase of the senior population will increase the national economic burden, and then the national economies of the advanced countries will be bankrupt.[2]

THE FIRST BIBLICAL TRUTH ON POPULATION

The first biblical truth is that the population should be increased up to filling the earth.

> God blessed them and said to them, "Be fruitful and increase in number; fill the earth." (Gen 1:28)

---

1. See United States Census Bureau.
2. Peterson, *Gray Dawn*, 72–93.

Production of Labor and "Fill the Earth and Subdue It"

Therefore, pregnancy control, abortion, and same-sex marriage should not be allowed because of their non-obedience against the will and provision of God for increasing population.

THE SECOND BIBLICAL TRUTH ON POPULATION

The second biblical truth is that policies for solving the senior population problem should be provided and implemented to keep the prosperity of the countries and the world for a long time.

> Honor your father and your mother, so that you may live long in the land the Lord your God is giving you. (Exod 20:5)

"You" in the verse above indicates the plural rather than the singular and should indicate the nation of Israel, and then "honor" means "provide policies for solving the problem of the father-and-mother generation."

The second issue of labor is the labor force

The labor force is a very significant element to maintain and increase the prosperity of the kingdom of God in terms of living life, including the economic life.

In the U.S., the labor force includes the population of age sixteen and above who have the capacity to work for a living. According to U.S. statistics of December 2019, the civilian noninstitutional population was 260.2 million, and the labor force 164.6 million, where the labor force participation ratio (the ratio of labor force over population) was 63.3%. The labor force of the world is estimated now at 4.9 billion.

THE BIBLICAL TRUTH ON THE LABOR FORCE

The biblical truth is that the labor force is the inevitable concept (element) to subdue the earth.

> Fill the earth and subdue it. (Gen 1:28)

For the Bible, there is a good story concerning the labor force. The book of Numbers of the Old Testament is the story about the census of Israelites wandering over the wildness after Exodus from the Egypt. Moses as the leader of the Israelites took two censuses in the wilderness.

> Take a census of the whole Israel community by their clans and families, listing every man by name, one by one. You and Aaron are to number by their divisions all the man in Israel twenty years old or more who are able to serve in the army. (Num 1:2–3)
>
> The total number was 603,550. (Num 1:46)
>
> After the plague the Lord said to Moses and Eleazar son of Aaron, the priest, "Take a census of the whole Israelite community by families—all those twenty years old or more who are able to serve in the army." (Num 26:1)
>
> The total number of men of Israel was 601,730. (Num 26:51)

Here, the serious question should be put openly: Why does God command to do two censuses at the beginning and at the end of the Israelites' wandering in the wildness for forty years? The answer is found when the Israelites occupy Jericho and Canaan under the leadership of Joshua.

Joshua occupied Jericho by using the strategy that God ordered without actual fighting.

> March around the city once with all the armed men. Do this for six days. Have seven priests carry trumpets of rams horns in front of the ark. On the seventh day, march around the city seven times, with the priests blowing the trumpets. (Josh 6:3–4)

The victory in occupying Jericho without actual fighting was earned because the Israelites demonstrated their strong military power of over 600,000 men of twenty years old or more.

The third issue of labor is employment.

Production of Labor and "Fill the Earth and Subdue It"

The U.S. employment total was 158.8 million in December 2019 and the unemployment 5.8 million. The employment-population ratio was 61.0% and the unemployment-labor force rate was 3.5%.

There are four problems related to employment, namely, employment labor productivity, human capital, discrimination, and income inequality and poverty.

The first employment issue is employment labor productivity.

How much the employed labor produces is a very important factor for the growth of the economy. The U.S. employment labor productivity was $137,777.78 in December 2019 and has increased about 2% every year, which is analyzed as moderate.

THE BIBLICAL TRUTH ON EMPLOYMENT LABOR PRODUCTIVITY

This biblical truth is:

> Slaves, obey your earthly masters with respect and fear, and with sincerity of heart, just as you would obey Christ. (Eph 6:5)

As employees work their assignments with respect and fear and sincerity of heart, their productivity increases for the growth of the economy.

The second employment issue is human capital.

Capital as one of the major production factors, including two kinds, namely, physical capital and human capital. Physical capital includes buildings, machines, tools, funds, etc., and human capital includes abilities, skills, experiences, etc.

After World War II, the economies of the two defeated countries, Germany and Japan, recovered in a few of years, called the Rhine River Economic Miracle and the Tokyo Economic Miracle. The factors producing those miracles were the human capital that the two countries produced and maintained before World War II.

THE BIBLICAL TRUTH ON HUMAN CAPITAL

The biblical truth is that human capital is increased and maintained through education and training.

> Fathers, do not exasperate your children; instead, bring them up in the training and instruction of the Lord. (Eph 6:4)

The third employment issue is discrimination.

Title VII of the U.S. Civil Rights Act enacted in 1964 made it illegal to discriminate against someone on the basis of race, color, religion, national origin, or sex. The existence of the glass ceiling for promotion and disparity of earnings still has been common in general.[3]

U.S. statistics on medium weekly earnings in the third quarter of 2019 show discrimination by race, education, and sex.

	Male	Female
White	1,025	843
Black	768	683
Asian	1,360	1,138
Hispanic	757	661
College	1,573	1,229
High School	857	629

THE BIBLICAL TRUTH ON DISCRIMINATION

This biblical truth is that nondiscrimination is ordered absolutely.

> My brother, as believers in our glorious Lord Jesus Christ, don't show favoritism. (Jas 2:1)

> Have you not discriminated among yourselves and become judges with evil thoughts? (Jas 2:4)

The fourth employment issue is income inequality and poverty.

---

3. See United States Civil Rights Act 1964.

Production of Labor and "Fill the Earth and Subdue It"

In the U.S. the richest 1% of income ranking earned 20.2% of the national gross income (GNI), while the low income earners, 50% of the income ranking, earned only 13.0% of GNI.

The World Bank puts the poverty line at $1.90 (2011 purchasing power parity) per day for the living. In the world population, 9.5% of the total, 702 million, live under the poverty line. The population under the poverty line are 4.1%, 5.6%, 13.5%, and 35.2% of the East Asia and Pacific regions, of the Latin America and Caribbean regions, of the South Asian region, and of the Sub-Africa region.[4]

The famous French economist Thomas Piketty has argued in his best-seller book titled *Capital in the Twenty-First Century* that the asset wealth of rich people has grown faster than the Gross Domestic Product, which is the basis of income inequality and poverty.[5]

There are three major political philosophies concerning income inequality and poverty, namely, liberalism, utilitarianism, and libertarianism.

Liberalism (egalitarianism) holds that every human being has equal rights, and then income inequality and poverty should be solved as society's corporate project.[6]

Utilitarianism argues that the main objective of society should be the maximization of the happiness of the most people. Utilitarianists pursue the implementation of workers' participation and greater equality of income by the community for the purpose of the maximization of happiness.[7]

Libertarianism maintains that everybody has his own individual liberty entitled both in birth and transfer, and then income inequality and poverty should be reduced by private charity programs rather than public assistance.[8]

---

4. See World Bank.
5. Piketty, *Capital in Twenty-First Century*, 336–70, 430–70.
6. Rawls, *Theory of Justice*.
7. Bentham, *Principles of Morals*, 1–10; Mill, *Utilitarianism*, 6–26.
8. Nozick, *Anarchy, State, and Utopia*, 3–25.

THE FIRST BIBLICAL TRUTH ON INCOME INEQUALITY AND POVERTY

The first biblical truth is that poverty should be erased by hard working.

> A little sleep, a little slumber, a little folding of the hands to rest—and poverty will come on you like a bandit and scarcity like an armed man. (Prov 6:10–11)

This truth is in the libertarian assertion.

THE SECOND BIBLICAL TRUTH ON POVERTY

The second biblical truth is that the aid and assistance should be given to the needy.

> He who despises his neighbor sins, but blessed is he who is kind to the needy. (Prov 14:21)

> He who oppresses the poor shows contempt for their Maker, but whoever is kind to the needy honors God. (Prov 14:31)

This truth is in liberalism (egalitarianism).

CHAPTER 7

Production of Capital and "Your Young Men Will See Visions"

(Joel 2:28)

THE NEXT ECONOMIC SUBJECT of production is the production expansion of capital.

Two major production factors (inputs) are labor and capital, as illustrated by production function.

Karl Marx argued in his historic book titled *Das Kapital* that all production value is produced by labor, only as demonstrated in labor value theory.[1] However, production value is to be produced and implemented not only by labor but also by capital, in addition to the raw materials.

Capital includes buildings, machines, tools, capital finances, etc., including all nonlabor inputs besides the raw materials. Capital is to be traded in the capital market, so called the loanable fund market, in which the loanable fund is the income left over after the income is spent for all kinds of consumption. In the capital market (the loanable fund market), the supply of capital is savings, while the demand for capital is investments. And the price of capital is the interest rate.

---

1. Marx, *Kapital*, 62–70.

There are two issues concerning the production expansion of capital (the capital market, the loanable fund market), namely, savings as the supply of capital and investments as the demand for capital.

The first issue of the capital market is savings as the supply of capital.

The saving rate should be increased for the increase in the production expansion of capital. However, for the U.S., the personal saving rate and the gross saving rate have been in the phenomenon of the steady state over the last three decades.

	1990	2000	2019
Personal Saving Rate	8.8%	4.2%	7.6%
Gross Saving Rate	19.0%	20.5%	17.0%

THE BIBLICAL TRUTH ON SAVING

This biblical truth is that saving is emphasized as the necessary and sufficient source of the living.

> You are to take every kind of food that is to be eaten and store it away as food for you and for them. (Gen 6:21).

The second issue of the capital market is investment.

Because investment is an important issue of the capital market, there are several issues on investments as the demand for the capital market.

The first issue of investment is the management of the investment.

Henry Fayol, a famous scholar on management, listed six functions of investment management, namely, forecasting, planning, organizing, commanding, coordinating, and controlling.[2]

---

2. Fayol, *Administration industrielle et générale*.

Production of Capital and "Your Young Men Will See Visions"

THE FIRST BIBLICAL TRUTH ON INVESTMENT MANAGEMENT

This biblical truth is that the vision, purpose, and objective of the investment should be challenging and distinctive, as poured from above.

> And afterward, I will pour my Spirit on all people. Your sons and daughters will prophesy, your old men will dream dreams, your young men will see visions. (Joel 2:28)

The visions are the vision, the dreams are the purpose, and the prophecy is the objective.

THE SECOND BIBLICAL TRUTH ON INVESTMENT MANAGEMENT

The second biblical truth is that the management of investment should be processed in the right direction with powerful decisions.

> Be strong and very courageous. Be careful to obey all the law my servant Moses gave you; do not turn from it to the right or to the left. (Josh 1:7)

THE THIRD BIBLICAL TRUTH ON INVESTMENT MANAGEMENT

The third biblical truth is that the management of investment should be controlled by the truth from above over time.

> The mind of sinful man is death, but the mind controlled by the Spirit is life and peace. (Rom 8:6)

The second issue of investment is on the technology development by investment.

The development of the national economy has been implemented by the development of technology by investment over time. This is true for the case of U.S. national economic development history.

The economic growth of a nation should be measured by the gross domestic product (GDP) of that nation. The United States's GDP was $300 billion in 1900 and decreased to $57 billion in 1933 due to the Great Depression. It recovered to $347 billion in 1951 and then increased continuously to $1 trillion in 1969, $10 trillion in 2000, $20 trillion in 2018, and $20 trillion in 2019. The U.S. GDP shows enormous economic size as one-fourth of the world GDP of $80 trillion.

What have the main sources been for the great expansion of the U.S. economy for the twentieth and twenty-first centuries? The answer articulated by most economists is that investment in technologies has increased the productivity and then the growth of the national economy.

It is true that most technologies utilized for the national economy have originated in the U.S. economy for the last two centuries. They have included electrical technology in the 1900s, automobile technology in the 1910s, electrical technology in the 1920s, jet-engine technology in the 1950s and 1960s, and information technology in the late twentieth and early twenty-first centuries. The U.S. economy has invested about 15% of its GDP in the research and development of technology.

THE BIBLICAL TRUTH FOR TECHNOLOGY DEVELOPMENT

The biblical truth is that the seed has to be planted for growth, to be ready for expansion.

> He told them another parable: The kingdom of heaven is like a mustard seed, which a man took and planted in his field. Though it is the smallest of all the seeds, yet when it grows, it is the largest of garden plants and becomes a tree, so that the birds of the air come and perch in its branches. (Matt 13:31–32)
>
> He told them still another parable: The kingdom of heaven is like yeast that a woman took and mixed into

Production of Capital and "Your Young Men Will See Visions"

> a large amount of flour until it worked all through the dough. (Matt 13:33)

The third issue of capital investment is the sources of the investment (financial sources).

The financial sources in the capital market are three: assets, debts, and stocks.

The first source of investment is the asset of savings.

THE BIBLICAL TRUTH ON ASSETS

This biblical truth is:

> The kingdom of heaven is like treasure hidden in a field. When a man found it, he hid it again, and then in his joy went and sold all he had and bought that field. (Matt 13:44)

> Again the kingdom of heaven is like a merchant looking for fine pearls. When he found one of great value, he went away and sold everything he had and bought it. (Matt 13:45–46)

The second source of finance is debt by getting loans from banks and/or by issuing and selling bonds in the bond market.

There are four biblical truths concerning debt.

THE FIRST BIBLICAL TRUTH ON DEBT

This biblical truth is to put up no security of debt for others.

> My son, if you have put up security for your neighbor, if you have struck hands in pledge for another, if you have been trapped by what you said, ensnared by the words of your mouth. (Prov 6:1–2)

> Do not be a man who strikes hands in pledge or puts up security for debts. (Prov 22:26)

THE SECOND BIBLICAL TRUTH ON DEBT

The second biblical truth is the proper management of debt.

> So he called in each one of his master's debtors. (Luke 16:5)

THE THIRD BIBLICAL TRUTH ON DEBT

The third biblical truth is that debts are to be used to gain friends.

> I tell you, use the worldly wealth to gain friends for yourselves, so that when it is gone, you will be welcomed into the eternal dwellings. (Luke 16:9)

THE FOURTH BIBLICAL TRUTH ON DEBT

The fourth biblical truth is that debts are to be written off after a certain period of time.

> At the end of every seven years you must cancel debts. (Deut 15:1)

The third source of finance is stocks.

The most active source of financing the capital required in production is issuing stocks and putting stocks in the stock market to provide the capital for the management of enterprises.

In the present global finance markets, the capitalization of all the stocks is counted at about $800 trillion, which is ten times more than the present global Gross Domestic Products.

The history of the stock market goes back to the 1600s. At that time the European merchants of Dutch, England, France, Italy, etc. got permission to establish business entities for their governments and then provided the required capital either through issuing bonds and/or stocks paying dividends. Bonds are to be the certificates of debts or loans, but stocks are to be the shares of ownership of an enterprise.

Sharing originates in Christianity, whose truth is to love.

Production of Capital and "Your Young Men Will See Visions"

> But the fruit of the Spirit is love, . . . kindness, goodness (Gal 5:22–23)
>
> And do not forget to do good and to share with others for with such sacrifices God is pleased. (Heb 15:16)
>
> All the believers were one in heart and mind. No one claimed that any of his possessions was his own, but they shared everything they had. (Acts 4:32)

THE BIBLICAL TRUTH ON STOCKS

This biblical truth is that stock markets as the main sources of capital are argued to originate in Christian love, in sharing.

CHAPTER 8

Production Optimization and "He Sold All He Had and Bought That Field"

(Matt 13:44)

IT IS THE TRUTH that the expansion of production through increasing labor and capital is a necessity for the expansion of the present aspect of the kingdom of God. At the same time, the optimization of production is a very important concept for the proper arrangement of the present aspect of the kingdom of God.

The optimization of production is classified into two kinds: the optimization of production inputs and the optimization of production output.

OPTIMIZATION OF PRODUCTION INPUTS

The first kind is the optimization of production inputs (production factors), which means to find the optimum size of production inputs such as labor and capital in order to maximize the production function with the given constraint of the allowed budget and the market prices of the production inputs.

Production Optimization

The economic theory states that the optimization of production inputs (the optimum sizes of the production factors such as labor and capital) for the maximization of production is achieved as the marginal products of all the production inputs become equal. The concept of the productivity of the production factors is very important, which implies the amount of the production output is produced by employing the production input at the current level of technology. The equalization of the marginal products of the inputs as the condition for the optimization of the inputs implies that the inputs should be employed up to the point of maximum product by employing those inputs.

There are four biblical truths concerning the productivity of the production inputs.

The First Biblical Truth on Input Productivity

The first biblical truth is that seed should be planted into good soil for good fruits.

> A farmer went out to sow his seed. (Matt 13:3)
>
> Still other seed fell on good soil, where it produced a crop—a hundred, sixty, or thirty times what was sown. (Matt 13:8)

The seed as either the production input or God's righteousness has to be planted into good soil, or the good soul, for the expansion of either the crop or the present aspect of the kingdom of God.

The Second Biblical Truth on Input Productivity

The second biblical truth is that the good seed is to be planted in the field, and then the wheat is to be selected from the weeds for storing in the barn.

> The kingdom of heaven is like a man who sowed good seed in his field. (Matt 13:24)

> First collect the weeds and tie them in bundles to be burned; then gather the wheat and bring it into my barn. (Matt 13:30)

Either the good seed or God's righteousness should be planted and waited for until the harvest, and then the wheat or God's righteousness is collected into either the barn or the present aspect of the kingdom of God.

The Third Biblical Truth on Input Productivity

The third biblical truth is that the good tree results in good fruits.

> Likewise every good tree bears good fruit, but a bad tree bears bad fruit. (Matt 7:17)

Like the good soil and the good seed, the good tree produces the good fruit, in which the good tree is Jesus Christ.

The Fourth Biblical Truth on Input Productivity

The fourth biblical truth is that the good fruit is to be harvested from the branches attached to the good vine tree of Jesus, in which God is the good farmer.

> I am the true vine, and my father is the gardener. (John 15:1)

> I am the vine; you are the branches. If a man remains in me and I in him, he will bear much fruit; apart from me you can do nothing. (John 15:5)

THE OPTIMIZATION OF PRODUCTION OUTPUT

The optimum size of production output in the market is an important concept for market efficiency on the production side in terms of the increasing production surplus value. The economic theory on the optimization of production output states that the condition for the optimization of production output is that the marginal revenue equals the marginal cost. As the marginal revenue equals the marginal cost, profit is to be maximized, and production output is at the optimum size. The profit, which is the revenue minus the cost, is the ultimate concept for the optimization of production output.

There are three biblical truths concerning profits.

The First Biblical Truth on Profits

The first biblical truth is that profits are to be earned as the business is managed with all effort.

> All hard work brings a profit, but mere talk leads only to poverty. (Prov 14:23)
>
> She sees that her trading is profitable, and her lamp does not go out at night. (Prov 31:18)

Profits are to be earned with hard work, as spiritual profits can be achieved with hard effort in the present aspect of God's kingdom.

The Second Biblical Truth on Profits

The second biblical truth is that all one's own properties should be invested to get the valuable profit.

> The kingdom of heaven is like treasure hidden in a field. When a man found it, he hid it again, and then in his joy went and sold all he had and bought that field. (Matt 13:44)
>
> Again, the kingdom of heaven is like a merchant looking for fine pearls. When he found one of great value, he went away and sold everything he had and bought it. (Matt 13:45–46)

When the treasures and pearls of God's kingdom are found, they should be bought with all one's properties that one has.

The Third Biblical Truth on Profits

The third biblical truth is that the profitable products are to be chosen from all the products.

> One again, the kingdom of heaven is like a net that was let down into the lake and caught all kinds of fish. When it was full, the fishermen pulled it up on the shore. Then they sat down and collected the good fish in baskets, but threw the bad away. (Matt 13:47–48)

As the good fish are to be collected and the bad ones to be thrown away, God's righteousness should be chosen and any unrighteousness be cast away.

Prosperity in the kingdom of God is to be achieved through the biblical truths on planting seeds and on earning profits, as the prosperity of the production can result through the optimization of production inputs and production ouput.

CHAPTER 9

Consumption of Freedom and "You Are Free to Eat"

(Gen 2:16)

THE ECONOMY HAS THREE areas of the market, namely, production, consumption, and distribution. The U.S. GDP amounted to $22 trillion in 2019, of which $15 trillion (68.2% of the GDP) belonged to consumption. Hence, consumption is a very important subject for the growth of the national economy (GDP) over time.

Consumption in the glorious economic life has three subjects to be considered and analyzed. The first subject of consumption is consumption for utility, which is the answer to the question of maximizing the satisfaction of the consumption. The second subject is consumption of temptation, which is the answer to the question of tempted consumption. The third subject is consumption in the family, which is the answer to the question of proper family consumption.

Consumption for utility means to consume goods and services while getting maximum satisfaction (maximizing the utility function) with the allowed budget of income and the prices of commodities in the market. The economic theory states that the condition for consumption for utility is to equalize the marginal utilities of the commodities at the given prices in the market. The utilities of the commodities for consumption is the important concept indicating the maximum satisfaction brought by the commodities consumed, which are to be produced by consuming the commodities freely.

> And the Lord God made all kinds of trees grow out of the ground—trees that were pleasing to the eye and good for food. (Gen 2:9)

> The Lord God took the man and put him in the garden of Eden to work it and take care of it. And the Lord God commanded the man, "You are free to eat from any tree in the garden." (Gen 2:15–16)

The biblical word on consumption for utility (satisfaction) is that we are free to consume—the free consumption for utility. At this point, freedom in consumption for utility is a very critical concept for the consumption, for freedom in the Bible indicates a very significant meaning in terms of the evangelism. Freedom in the Bible indicates freedom from sin through the gospel.

> Then you will know the truth, and the truth will set you free. (John 8:32)

> If the Son sets you free, you will be free indeed. (John 8:36)

The real truth of freedom from sin has been taught by Paul in the Bible.

> You, my brothers, were called to be free. But do not use your freedom to indulge the sinful nature; rather, serve one another in love. The entire law is summed up in a single command: "Love your neighbor as yourself." (Gal 5:13–14)

Freedom from sin through Jesus Christ's cross and resurrection is not freedom for the satisfaction of bodily ambition, but freedom for serving each other with love, because the real aspect of love is possible from real freedom.

Are the real objectives of the creation and the salvation of human beings to be related to love? The creation of human beings in God's image and salvation through Jesus Christ provide the true freedom for true love.

Consumption of Freedom and "You Are Free to Eat"

> So God created man in his own image, in the image of God he created him; male and female he created them. (Gen 2:27)

> For God so loved the world that he gave his one and only Son, whoever believes in him shall not perish but have eternal life. (John 3:16)

In this understanding, "You are free to eat" indicates free consumption with love. Love has eight aspects in the Bible, as taught by Paul.

> But the fruit of the Spirit is love, joy, peace, patience, kindness, goodness, faithfulness, gentleness and self-control. Against such things there is no law. (Gal 5:22–23)

THE BIBLICAL TRUTH ON CONSUMPTION

This biblical truth is that free consumption has to be consumption with love, namely, the consumption bringing joy and thanks, the consumption producing peace, the consumption controlled with patience, the consumption helping the poor, the consumption doing goodness for the community, the consumption fulfilling obligations for the community, the consumption participating in the common interests, and the consumption cutting the nonnecessities.

CHAPTER 10

Consumption of Temptation and "You Must Not Eat from the Tree of the Knowledge of Good and Evil"

(Gen 2:17)

CONSUMPTION IS ONE OF the main sources of growth of the national economy. About two-thirds of the U.S. GDP ($22 trillion) occupies consumption (about 68%) so that the growth of the GDP comes from the expansion of consumption. However, the problem is that consumption has increased tremendously since the late twentieth century, beyond consumption for the necessity and sufficiency of lives. This phenomenon is called the consumption of temptation, which has two kinds, namely, consumerism and the consumption of calling evil as good.

CONSUMERISM

Consumption has increased tremendously on the scale of global perspective, not only in the advanced economies but also in the emerging and underdeveloped economies since the late twentieth century. James Twitchell, professor of economics at Florida State University, wrote the best-seller book titled *Lead Us Into*

Consumption of Temptation

Temptation (1999), which explains the phenomenon of consumerism in the United States' economy. He explains two phenomena of U.S. consumerism.[1]

The first phenomenon of U.S. consumerism is that there are many consumers spending their income to buy goods and services not for their necessity nor for their sufficiency but only for following the consumption pattern of their neighbors and friends who have higher positions than their own positions, in order to make their rankings higher than their present situation.

Twitchell estimates that this kind of consumerism is about 30% of total consumption in the United States.

The second phenomenon of consumerism is that national debt has increased tremendously, up to the point of harming the growth of the national economy for most advanced and emerging economies. The national debt of the U.S. is $22 trillion, composing 105% of the GDP in 2019. Japanese debt is $12 trillion, 267% of Japan's GDP. Global debt is $186 trillion, becoming 239% of the global GDP.

The First Biblical Truth on Consumerism

The first biblical truth is: "Do not consume for more than the necessity and sufficiency of lives."

> Why spend money on what is not bread, and your labor on what does not satisfy? Listen, listen to me, eat what is good, and your soul will delight in the richest of fare. (Isai 55:2)

By consuming for the necessity and sufficiency of lives, our souls will delight to the fullest.

The Second Biblical Truth on Consumerism

The second biblical truth is that to owe debt is not allowed in any circumstance.

---

1. Twitchell, *Lead Us into Temptation*, 271–86.

> Let no debt remain outstanding except the continuing debt to love one another, for he who loves his fellowman has fulfilled the law. (Rom 13:8)

> Love does no harm to its neighbor. Therefore love is the fulfillment of the law. (Rom 13:10)

Debts are not allowed in the Bible, except for the debts of love, because the fulfillment of all the laws is accomplished by love, as Jesus said on his mission in Matt 5:17.

> Do not think that I have come to abolish the Law or the Prophets; I have not come to abolish them but to fulfill them. (Matt 5:17)

The Third Biblical Truth on Consumerism

The third biblical truth is that security for the debts of others is forbidden in any circumstance.

> Do not be a man who strikes hands in pledge or puts up security for debts. (Prov 22:26)

Security for others' debts is the direct way to total bankruptcy on both sides.

CONSUMPTION FROM THE KNOWLEDGE OF GOOD AND EVIL

Adam and Eve were kicked out of the garden of Eden because they had eaten from the tree of the knowledge of good and evil (Gen 2:17, 3:6, 3:24).

Why did God prohibit Adam and Eve from eating from the tree of the knowledge of good and evil?

The answer is in Isa 5:20:

> Woe to those who call evil good and good evil, who put darkness for light and light for darkness, who put bitter for sweet and sweet for bitter.

Consumption of Temptation

Once human beings have gotten knowledge of good and evil, they take advantage of exchanging good and evil, light and darkness, and sweet and bitter: doing evil as good and criticizing good as evil, emphasizing darkness as light and belittling light as darkness, and receiving bitter as sweet and scorning sweet as bitter.

There are three biblical truths on consumption from the knowledge of good and evil.

THE FIRST BIBLICAL TRUTH ON CONSUMPTION FROM THE KNOWLEDGE OF GOOD AND EVIL

The first biblical truth is that the foolish enjoy dissolute consumption as good.

> A fool finds pleasure in evil conduct, but a man of understanding delights in wisdom. (Prov 10:23)

Evil consumption as good is very common in these days and foolish.

THE SECOND BIBLICAL TRUTH ON CONSUMPTION FROM THE KNOWLEDGE OF GOOD AND EVIL

The second biblical truth is that consumption in darkness appears as consumption in light, as Satan of darkness appears as an angel of light.

> And no wonder, for Satan himself masquerades as an angel of light. (2 Cor 11:14)

There are many cases for consumption in darkness as that in light.

THE THIRD BIBLICAL TRUTH ON CONSUMPTION FROM THE TREE OF THE KNOWLEDGE OF GOOD AND EVIL

The third biblical truth is that the full do not consume even sweet as bitter, but the hungry consume bitter as sweet.

> He who is full loathes honey, but to the hungry even what is bitter tastes sweet. (Prov 27:7)

The consumption of bitter as sweet or of sweet as bitter does depend upon fullness or hunger.

CHAPTER 11

Economy of the Family and "They Will Become One Flesh"

(Gen 2:24)

THE MAIN UNIT OF consumption is the family, including the individuals. The word *economy* originates from the Greek, combining two words, *oikos* and *nomia*. *Oikos* means "family" and *nomia* "management," implying that *economy* indicates management of the family.

The Bible teaches three areas concerning the consumption economy of the family, namely, fundamental biblical truths, living biblical truths, and Christian biblical truths.

FUNDAMENTAL BIBLICAL TRUTHS ON THE FAMILY ECONOMY

Then the Lord God made a woman from the rib he had taken out of the man, and he brought her to the man. (Gen 2:22)

For this reason a man will leave his father and mother and be united with his wife, and they will become one flesh. The man and his wife were both naked, and they felt no shame. (Gen 2:24–25)

The First Fundamental Biblical Truth on the Family Economy

The first fundamental biblical truth is that the man and his wife as a family should leave the father and mother.

Leaving the parents has the crucial implication of the family starting an independent new life with its own decision-making.

However, the economic dependence of the family upon the parent economy has resulted in a dependence of family life, which has generated the decay of the life of the family over time.

The Second Fundamental Biblical Truth on the Family Economy

The second fundamental biblical truth is that the man and wife become one flesh, which indicates that every activity of the family should be made in joint decision-making, without the individual actions from one's own secret.

The Bible supports joint accounts rather than independent accounts in banking especially.

The good points of joint accounts are (1) convenience, (2) simple legal affairs, and (3) exact oversight, while the bad points are (1) nonindependence, (2) inequality, and (3) messy breakups. However, the family should have financial union for a happier family life, more than ever.

The Third Fundamental Biblical Truth on the Family Economy

The third fundamental biblical truth is that the family economy should be transparent in all aspects of economic activity.

Economy of the Family and "They Will Become One Flesh"

> The man and his wife were naked, and they felt no shame.
> (Gen 2:15)

There cannot be any secret in all the economic phenomena of the family, even for the good purpose of economic prospects.

Transparency is a very important subject, not only in the family economy but also in all areas of the economy, such as the national, business, and individual economies.

Transparency in the dictionary definition implies openness, communication, and accountability. Transparency International (TI), founded in 1993, defines transparency as freedom from corruption. TI has reported the Corruption Perception Index (CPI) of countries every year since 1993. A CPI of 100 indicates the most transparency, and a CPI of 0 shows the most corruption.

According to TI's 2019 report, New Zealand and Denmark had a CPI of 87 as the most transparent countries of the world. Great Britain was the twelfth, Japan the twentieth, the U.S. the twenty-sixth, South Korea the thirty-ninth, and China the eightieth transparent country of the world.[1]

The transparency of nations is a significant concept, not only in the domestic economic, social, and cultural areas but also in international affairs around the world. However, it should be recognized clearly that all kinds of corruption have been initiated into the nontransparency of the family economy.

LIVING BIBLICAL TRUTHS ON THE FAMILY ECONOMY

After the fall for eating from the tree of the knowledge of good and evil, the man and woman have to follow God's commands, which are the living biblical truths on the family economy. There are three living biblical truths, including two for the woman and one for the man.

---

1. See Transparency International.

The First Living Biblical Truth to the Woman

The first living biblical truth is that the woman gives birth to children with pains, increasing the population of human beings.

> To the woman he said, "I will greatly increase your pains in childbearing; with pain you will give birth to children." (Gen 3:16)

The world population and the birth rate have been decreasing since the late twentieth century. The World Fact Book of the United States CIA shows that the crude birth rates of Angola and Nigeria were 44.20 as the 1st and 2nd, the U.S. 12.50 as the 158th, Great Britain 12.10 as the 166th, Japan 7.70 as the 223rd, China 12.30 as the 161st, and South Korea 8.30 as the 220th.

This trend of a lowering birth rate around the world has been argued by most world population experts and realized every year over time.

The Second Living Biblical Truth to the Woman

The second living biblical truth is that the woman manages the family lives according to the man's (husband's) commands.

> You desire will be for your husband, and he will rule over you. (Gen 3:16)

The husband is the leader of the family, while the woman follows the husband's leadership with the management of all kinds of the family life.

The Third Living Biblical Truth to the Man

The third living biblical truth is that the income of the family should be earned by the man until he dies.

> Cursed is the ground because of you; through painful toil you will eat of it all the days of you life. It will produce thorns and thistles for you, and you will eat the plants of

Economy of the Family and "They Will Become One Flesh"

> the field. By the sweat of your brow you will eat your food until you return to the ground, since from it you were taken. (Gen 3:17–19)

Even if the wife's share of the household income has been increasing continuously over time, the management of the household's income could be managed in recognition of the man as the head of the family.

CHRISTIAN BIBLICAL TRUTHS ON THE FAMILY

The New Testament teaches Christian biblical truths on family life once we become Christians, after we believe the salvation by Jesus Christ and accept Jesus Christ as Lord.

There are two relationships in Christian family life. One relationship is the husband and the wife, while the other relationship is the parents and the children

The First Christian Biblical Truth on the Husbands-Wives Relationship

The first Christian biblical truths are that the husbands love their wives and the wives submit to their husbands.

> Husbands, love your wives, just as Christ loved the church and gave himself up for her. (Eph 5:25)

> Wives, submit to your husbands as to the Lord. (Eph 5:22)

The husbands' love to their wives should be the love of giving themselves up for their wives just as Christ gave himself up for the church. The husbands can provide joy, peace, patience, kindness, goodness, faithfulness, gentleness, and self-control.

And the wives' submission to their husbands should be the submission of the church to Jesus Christ as its Savior, like the martyrs.

The Second Christian Biblical Truth on the Parents-Children Relationship

The second Christian biblical truth is that the parents teach their children, and the children honor their parents.

> Fathers, do not exasperate your children; instead, bring them up in the training and instruction of the Lord. (Eph 6:4)

> Children, obey your parents in the Lord, for this is right. "Honor your father and mother"—which is the first commandment with the promise—"that it may go well with you and that you may enjoy long life on the earth." (Eph 6:1–3)

A recent survey by the Pew Research Center shows that three out of five of the millennials generation born between 1981 and 1996 in the United States do not attend church weekly.[2] Most millennials went to church weekly until leaving home for college because they followed their parents' Christian life pattern. However, as they left home for college, they did not go to church weekly under their own life pattern. This phenomenon argues for their parents' non-biblical teaching of their children concerning the Christian life of the family.

Professor of psychology Baumrind argues that there are four different types of parents' teaching of their children. She indicates that there are two elements, namely, control and love, in the parents' teaching of their children, and lists four types of the parents' teaching: (1) an authoritative style of strong control and strong love, (2) an authoritarian style of strong control but weak love, (3) a permissive style of weak control but strong love, and (4) an uninvolved style of weak control and weak love.[3]

She asserts that the authoritarian style leads to children of a nonsocial attitude, the permissive style to children involved with their own satisfaction, and the uninvolved style to children of non-independence. The authoritative style is to lead to the children with

2. Pew Research Center.
3. Baumrind, "Child Care Practices."

Economy of the Family and "They Will Become One Flesh"

creativity, which is to assert Christian biblical truth, saying that the parents teach their children with the training and the instruction of the Lord, and that they put efforts into making their children not be exasperated.

In terms of the children's attitude toward their parents, the children should obey and honor their parents. These days, taking care of the parents is not easy and costs a lot. Hence, taking care of the parents by the children has decreased recently in most countries. However, the Bible teaches that as the children honor their parents, they live long, implying that taking care of the senior generation leads to the longer life of that nation.

CHAPTER 12

Social Welfare Function and "Be Holy, Because I Am Holy"

(Lev 11:45)

THE GLORIOUS ECONOMIC LIFE is composed of three areas, namely, production, consumption, and distribution. In these three areas, distribution is a significant subject, because it includes the incomes of the participants in production, such as payments to suppliers, wages to laborers, salaries to managers, dividends to investors, etc. Therefore, distribution is related to economic principles and at the same time to philosophical value theories.

Distribution should be analyzed with general equilibrium theory as the economic theory, together with social welfare function as the philosophical value theory.[1]

The general equilibrium theory has two areas, namely, the production area with many production inputs (factors) and many production outputs, and the exchange area with many production outputs and many consumers. The main principle applied to these two areas is the efficiency principle, which states that "no one can be better off unless someone else is made worse off."

---

1. Edgeworth, *Mathematical Physics*; Pareto, *Manual di economia Politica*.

Social Welfare Function and "Be Holy, Because I Am Holy"

General equilibrium in production produces a production possibility curve based on the efficiency principle, and at the same time, general equilibrium in exchange results in the utility possibility curve being applied by the efficiency principle. In other words, any point in the production possibility curve and any point in the utility possibility curve are the optimum points of production and exchange for consumption, satisfying the efficiency principle.

At this point, the actual point of production and the actual point of exchange for consumption are to be determined by the social welfare function, which is the philosophical value system chosen by the people of the nation and/or society.

Concerning the social welfare function, there are three main philosophical value systems, namely, liberalism, utilitarianism, and libertarianism.

LIBERALISM

Liberalism states that everybody has an equal right to be protected.

John Rawls (1921–2002), professor of philosophy at Harvard University, argued for two principles of liberalism in his book titled *A Theory of Justice*: the first principle is that everyone has an equal right for protection; the second principle is that inequality is allowed for only two cases, for (1) the equality of opportunity given and (2) the greatest benefit of the least advantaged members.

UTILITARIANISM

Utilitarianism, proposed by Jeremy Bentham and John Stuart Mill, argues for the most happiness for everyone in the community.

Utilitarianism suggests three ways for the improvement of distribution: (1) supplying more production, (2) increasing worker participation, and (3) trying for a more equal distribution of income.

LIBERTARIANISM

Libertarianism argues for the entitlement of property rights.

Robert Nozick, professor of philosophy at Harvard University, defends his entitlement theory, which says that the persons who acquired a holding through the principle of justice in acquisition and in transfer are entitled to the holding.

The glorious life in the present aspect of the kingdom of God (KG) is to live the rule by God in terms of his actual characteristics, such as glory, holiness, righteousness, grace and love, truthfulness, and wisdom. It also indicates the three Ps of life: the Purpose of life is glory, the Policies of life are holiness and righteousness, and the Processes of life are love, truth, and wisdom.

The Biblical Truth on Glory

This biblical truth is that glory is the appearance and fullness of God.

> And the glory of the Lord appeared to all the people. (Lev 9:23)

> For the glory of the Lord filled his temple. (1 Kgs 8:11)

The glory of God indicates his greatness and his authority.

Human beings, as the children of God and as people of the kingdom of God, should live the glorious economic life expressing clearly the glory of God.

The Biblical Truth on Holiness and Righteousness

This biblical truth is "be holy and be righteous (perfect)."

> Therefore be holy, because I am holy. (Lev 11:45)

> Be perfect, therefore, as your heavenly Father is perfect. (Matt 5:48)

The holiness of God is his wholeness, his perfection, and the freedom from evil.

Social Welfare Function and "Be Holy, Because I Am Holy"

Righteousness is uprightness in accordance with God's standard and has three values, namely, justice, equality, and integrity, which represent libertarianism, liberalism, and utilitarianism, respectively.

The Biblical Truth on Justice (Libertarianism)

This biblical truth is being just and right for all the people.

> David reigned over all Israel, doing what was just and right for all his people. (2 Sam 8:15)
>
> I will put my Spirit on him and he will bring justice to the nations. (Isa 42:1)

The Biblical Truth on Equality (Liberalism)

This biblical truth is to judge not partially but fairly.

> To show partiality in judging is not good. (Prov 24:23)
>
> Speak up and judge fairly; defend the rights of the poor and needy. (Prov 31:9)

The Biblical Truth on Integrity (Utilitarianism)

This biblical truth is that the Lord is faithful and loves the integrity.

> All the ways of the Lord are loving and faithful for those who keep the demands of his covenant. (Ps 25:10)
>
> The works of his hands are faithful and just; all his precepts are trustworthy. (Ps 111:7)
>
> I know, my God, that you test the heart and are pleased with integrity. (1 Chron 29:17)

THE ECONOMY OF THE KINGDOM OF GOD

The Biblical Truths on Love, Truth, and Wisdom

These biblical truths are that love is the fruit of the Spirit, the truth is Jesus Christ, and wisdom is the fear of God.

> But the fruit of the Spirit is love, joy, peace, patience, kindness, goodness, faithfulness, gentleness and self-control. (Gal 5:22–23)
>
> Jesus answered, "I am the way and the truth and the life. No one comes to the Father except through me." (John 14:6)
>
> The fear of the Lord is the beginning of wisdom. (Prov 9:10)

CHAPTER 13

Economic Policies and "The Noble Man Makes Noble Plans"

(Isa 32:8)

CAPITALISM HAS PROVIDED THE progress and prosperity of the global economy the last four centuries. However, capitalism is not a perfect economic system but is claimed as the best thought for the growth of national economies, even with its failures. There are two failures of capitalism, namely, market failures and business fluctuation failures.

Market failures are the microeconomic ones, while business fluctuation failures are the macroeconomic ones.

The failures of capitalism have tried to be corrected by government, which has implemented economic policies.

Market failures include externalities, market power, public goods, poverty, and asymmetric information.

The externalities of market failures are the external outputs of a positive value (positive externalities: education) or of a negative value (negative externalities: air or water pollution).

Negative externalities produce social costs in addition to individual costs, which are to be controlled either by setting environmental pollution standards or by creating environmental pollution taxes.

The market powers of market failures are monopoly, oligopoly, and monopolistic competition. Market power results in higher prices, fewer products, less competition, and the deadweight loss of market efficiency, which is composed of the sum of the consumer's and producer's surpluses.

There are three ways to control the market power of market failures: anti-trust acts, regulations, and public enterprises.

There are two standards for classifying goods and services (G&S) in the market. Excludability is one standard, and rivalry another standard. The G&S with both excludability and rivalry are the private ones, like most consumption G&S. The G&S with excludability but without rivalry are the natural monopolies like fire protection. The G&S without excludability but with rivalry are the common resources like the fish in the sea. The G&S with neither excludability nor rivalry are the public G&S like national defense, public roads, etc.

The public G&S are market failures.

Poverty is a market failure. The domestic policies for poverty reduction are welfare programs, such as the minimum wage, negative income taxes, in-kind transfers, work incentives, etc. In addition, international aids and work incentive projects help poverty reduction in international perspectives.

Asymmetric information is a market failure. There are two cases of asymmetric information, namely, principals versus agents and sellers versus buyers. The classic example of principals versus agents is the corporation, where the stockholders as the principals have less information than the managers as the agents. Another example is the used cars dealerships, where the used car dealers as the sellers have more information on the used cars than the customers as the used cars buyers.

For solving the asymmetric information of market failures, public information acts and some information control regulations are to be instituted and implemented.

The market economy of capitalism produces not only the market failures as mentioned above but, at the same time, results in business cycles or business fluctuations. There are two phases of business fluctuations, such as recovery and recession, in terms of

Economic Policies and "The Noble Man Makes Noble Plans"

the increasing phase and the decreasing phase of the Gross Domestic Products (GDP). Recession is defined as a phase of the negative growth of the GDP in two consecutive quarters, and recession with more than minus 10% for one year or more is called depression.

For the U.S. economy, there was one depression in the 1930s and five recessions since the late twentieth century, namely, the oil recessions in 1973 and 1982, the stagflation in 1991, the information technology bubble burst in 2001, and the housing bubble burst in 2009.

There are two economic policies for solving recessions: one is fiscal policies, and the other monetary policies.

Fiscal policies for solving the recession are to be implemented by the government after being approved by Congress, whose main elements are the reduction of taxes and increases in government expenditures such as for infrastructure. Tax reduction policies result in increases of consumption and investments of businesses. The infrastructural investment expenditures bring multiplier effects to the growth of the GDP through increases in investments, incomes, consumption, etc.

The second economic policy for economic recovery from recession is the monetary (financial) policy, which increases or decreases the amount of money in the circulation. The Federal Reserve Board as the central bank of the United States has the power of controlling the amount of money in the market by three tools, namely, changes of the discount interest rate, open market operation, and changes of the reserve requirements.

The discount interest rate is the interest rate to be charged to city banks for borrowing money from the Federal Reserve Board. The open market operation (quantitative ease) is the buying and selling of bonds in the bond market. The reserve requirement is the minimum reserve required for bank loans. The amount of money in the market is to be increased or decreased by a lower or higher discount rate by the Federal Reserve Board. Buying or selling bonds in the bond market by the FDB tends to increase or decrease the money in circulation. City banks can increase or decrease more loans through decreasing or increasing the reserve requirements by the FDB.

There are four biblical truths concerning economic policies in general.

THE FIRST BIBLICAL TRUTH ON ECONOMIC POLICIES

The first biblical truth is that economic policy is to be determined by the majority rule in voting.[1]

> The lot is cast into the lap, but its every decision is from the Lord. (Prov 16:33)

> Then they cast lots, and the lot fell to Matthias; so he was added to the eleven apostles. (Acts 1:26)

THE SECOND BIBLICAL TRUTH ON ECONOMIC POLICIES

The second biblical truth is that economic policies are to be planned by persons with professional knowledges and wisdom.

> But the noble man makes noble plans, and by noble deeds he stands. (Isa 32:8)

THE THIRD BIBLICAL TRUTH ON ECONOMIC POLICIES

The third biblical truth is that the policies are to be fit to God's plans, to be better and to be eternal.

> I know that you can do all things; no plan of yours can be thwarted. (Job 42:2)

> God had planned something better for us so that only together with us would they be made perfect. (Heb 11:40)

---

1. Condorcet, "Essay on the Application"; Arrow, *Social Choice*.

Economic Policies and "The Noble Man Makes Noble Plans"

> But the plans of the Lord stand firm forever, the purposes of his heart through all generations. (Ps 33:11)

THE FOURTH BIBLICAL TRUTH ON ECONOMIC POLICIES

The fourth biblical truth is that policies are to be implemented through consultation, wisdom, encouragement, generosity, diligence, cheerfulness, and commitment to God.

> Plans fail for lack of counsel, but with many advisers they succeed. (Prov 15:22)

> If it is encouraging, let him encourage; if it is contributing to the needs of others, let him give generously; if it is leadership, let him govern diligently; if it is showing mercy, let him do it cheerfully. (Rom 12:8)

> Commit to the Lord whatever you do, and your plans will succeed. (Prov 16:3)

CHAPTER 14

The Kingdom of God in the Bible: The Glorious Biblical Life

JESUS CHRIST CAME TO this world for the purpose of teaching about the kingdom of God (KG; kingdom of heaven, KH), including salvation into the KG. In the four Gospels he mentioned the KG in seventy-three verses (Matthew, thirty-five verses; Mark, nine verses; Luke, twenty-five verses; and John, four verses).

The KG is the kingdom ruled by God. Here are two questions to be asked concerning the real aspect of the KG. The first question is "With what is the KG ruled by God?" and the second question is "How are our lives living the rule by God in the KG?"

To answer these two fundamental questions concerning the KG, Jesus Christ taught the KG by (1) parables (KG production functions) and (2) exposition (themes of the words of God; attributes or characteristics of God).

KG PRODUCTION FUNCTIONS

In the parables, Jesus explained the KG using the parables of "like," which produce the outputs by using the inputs, called the *production function*. The production function is the economic concept that explains that the production output is produced as a function of production inputs (production factors), such as raw materials, labor, capital, etc. Let them be called the KG production functions.

The outputs of the KG production functions are the outputs of the words of God with which God rules over the KG and at the same time with which we live his ruling by submitting to and participating in the KG production functions.

There are fifteen parables in four Gospels explaining the KG by Jesus. Let's apply the KG production functions to the fifteen parables.

First KG Production Function

This function is that the crop is produced by scattering the seed in the good soil.

> When anyone hears the message about the kingdom. . . . But the one who received the seed that fell on good soil is the man who hears the word and understand it. He produces the crop yielding a hundred, sixty, or thirty times what was sown. (Matt 13:19, 23)

God rules over the KG with the output of the word of God (WG) like the crop yielding a hundred, sixty, or thirty times produced by scattering seed as the input of the WG in the good soil, as in our spiritual soul. We live his ruling with the output of the WG like the crop yielding abundantly by submitting to and participating in the seed being scattered as the input of the WG in the good soil, as in the spiritual soul that we provide.

Second KG Production Function

This function is that the wheat is produced for being gathered, grown by sowing good seed in the field.

> The kingdom of heaven is like a man who sowed good seed in his field. (Matt 13:24)

God rules over the KG with the output of the WG like the wheat grown being gathered and the weeds grown being burned, by sowing good seed as the input of the WG in God's field. We live God's rulings with the output of the WG like the wheat gathered by submitting to and participating in being sowed as good seed as the input of the WG, being gathered as wheat grown, and being thrown out as weeds during the harvest, as the output of the WG.

Third KG Production Function

This function is that a big tree is produced by taking and planting a mustard seed.

> The kingdom of heaven is like a mustard seed which a man took and planted in his field. (Matt 13:31)

God rules over the KG with the output of the WG like a big tree where the birds perch, by taking and planting the mustard seed as the input of the WG. We live his ruling with the output of the WG like the big tree by submitting to and participating into being taken and planted as a mustard seed as the input of the WG.

Fourth KG Production Function

This function is that the dough is made big by taking and mixing the yeast.

> The kingdom of heaven is like yeast that a woman took and mixed into a large amount of flour until it worked all through the dough. (Matt 13:33)

God rules over the KG with the output of the WG like the dough, by taking and mixing yeast into the flour as the input of the WG as into our spiritual soul. We live his ruling with the output of the WG like the dough by submitting to and participating into being taken and mixed as yeast as the input of the WG into the flour, as into our spiritual soul that we provide.

Fifth KG Production Function

This function is that the treasure is earned by finding, hiding, selling all one has, and buying the field.

> The kingdom of heaven is like treasure hidden in a field. When a man found it, he hid it again, and then in his joy went and sold all he had and bought that field. (Matt 13:44)

God rules over the KG with the output of the WG like the treasure earned by finding, hiding, selling all one has, and buying the field. We live his ruling with the output of the WG like treasure earned by submitting to and participating into being found, hidden, sold, and bought, as the investment in our spiritual soul.

Sixth KG Production Function

This function is that the fine pearls are earned by finding, selling everything, and buying it.

> Again, the kingdom of heaven is like a merchant looking for fine pearls. When he found one of great value, he went away and sold everything he had and bought it. (Matt 13:45)

God rules over the KG with the output of the WG like the fine pearl earned by finding, selling everything, and buying it. We live his ruling with the output of the WG like the fine pearls by submitting to and participating in being found, sold, and bought as the investment in our spiritual soul.

Seventh KG Production Function

This function is that the good fish are earned by pulling up all kinds of fish by a net, collecting the good fish, and throwing away the bad.

> Once again, the kingdom of heaven is like a net that was let down into the lake and caught all kinds of fish. When it was full, the fisherman pulled it up on the shore. Then

they sat down and collected the good fish in baskets, but
threw the bad away. (Matt 13:47–48)

God rules over the KG with the output of the WG like the good fish earned by pulling up all kinds of fish by a net, collecting the good fish, and throwing away the bad. We live his ruling with the output of the WG like the good fish by submitting to and participating into being pulled up like all kinds of fish by a net, collected with the good fish, and thrown away with the bad in the selection for our spiritual soul.

Eighth KG Production Function

This function is that new and old treasures are shown by being brought out from JC's house.

> Therefore every teacher of the law who has been instructed about the kingdom of heaven is like the owner of a house who brings out of his storeroom new treasures as well as old. (Matt 13:52)

God rules over the KG with the output of the WG like the new and old treasures brought and shown by the owner of the house. We live his ruling with the output of the WG like the new and old treasures by submitting to and participating in being brought and shown as the new and old treasures, as the new and old output of the WG.

Ninth KG Production Function

This function is that accounts are settled by forgiving.

> Therefore, the kingdom of heaven is like a king who wanted to settle accounts with his servants. . . . The servant master took pity on him, canceled the debt and let him go. . . . But he refused. Instead, he went off and had the man thrown into prison until he could pay the debt. . . . This is how my heavenly Father will treat each of you

> unless you forgive your brother from your heart. (Matt 18:23, 27, 30, 35)

God rules over the KG with the output of the WG like the accounts forgiven. We live God's ruling with the output of the WG like the accounts forgiven by submitting to and participating in forgiving our accounts to our servants as God forgives our accounts.

Tenth KG Production Function

This function is that hiring and paying are implemented by agreement.

> For the kingdom of heaven is like a landowner who went out early in the morning to hire men to work in his vineyard. He agreed to pay them a denarius for the day and sent them into his vineyard. . . . Take your pay and go. I want to give the man who was hired last the same as I gave you. Don't I have the right to do what I want with my own money? . . . So the last will be first, and the first will be last. (Matt 20:1–2,14–15, 16)

God rules over the KG with the output of the WG like hiring and paying in agreement. We live his ruling with the output of the WG like hiring and paying in agreement by submitting to and participating in being hired and paid in agreement, as the entrance into the KG without order of sequence by God's allowance.

Eleventh KG Production Function

This function is that we are made ready for a wedding banquet by wearing wedding clothes.

> The kingdom of heaven is like a king who prepared a wedding banquet for his son. . . . Friend, he asked, how did you get in here without wedding clothes? The man was speechless. . . . For many are invited, but few are chosen. (Matt 22:2,12,14)

God rules over the KG with the output of the WG like the wedding banquet being attended by the invited wearing the wedding clothes. We live God's kingdom with the output of the WG like the wedding banquet for the invited by submitting to and participating in attending, wearing the wedding clothes as wearing the spiritual mind.

Twelfth KG Production Function

This function is that five wise virgins went into the wedding banquet by taking oil in jars with their lamps.

> At that time the kingdom of heaven will be like ten virgins who took their lamps and went out to meet the bridegroom.... The wise (five), however, took oil in jars along with their lamps.... At midnight the cry rang out: Here's the bridegroom! Come out to meet him! ... The virgins who were ready went in with him to the wedding banquet. And the door was shut. (Matt 25:1, 4, 6, 10)

God rules over the KG with the output of the WG like the five wise virgins going into the wedding banquet by taking oil in jars with their lamps. We live his ruling with the output of the WG like the five wise virgins by submitting to and participating in going to the wedding banquet with oil in jars and lamps at the entrance, as the preparation for the wedding banquet with the Lord as the bridegroom.

Thirteenth KG Production Function

This function is that the men with five or two talents brought five or two talents more by working and gaining five or two talents.

> Again, it [the KH] will be like a man going on a journey, who called his servants entrusted his property to them. To one he gave five talents of money, to another two talents, and to another one talent, each according to his ability. Then he went on his journey.... After a long time the master of those servants returned and settled

accounts with them. The man who had received the five talents brought the other five. Master, he said, you entrusted me with five talents. See, I have gained five more. ... The man with two talents also came. Master, he said, you entrusted me with two talents; see, I have gained two more. (Matt 25:14–15, 19–20, 22)

God rules over the KG with the output of the WG like the men with five or two talents bringing five or two talents more by working. We live his ruling with the output of the WG like the men with five or two talents by submitting to and participating in bringing five or two talents more by working, as the output of the WG increased double by working.

Fourteenth KG Production Function

This function is that grain is earned in the harvest by scattering seed on the ground.

This is what the kingdom of God is like. A man scatters seed on the ground. . . . As soon as the grain is ripe, he puts the sickle to it, because the harvest has come. (Mark 4:26, 29)

God rules over the KG with the output of the WG like the grain earned in the harvest by scattering seed as the input of the WG on the ground, as on our spiritual mind. We live his ruling with the output of the WG like the grain harvested by submitting to and participating in being scattered seed as the input of the WG on the ground, as on our spiritual mind.

Fifteenth KG Production Function

This function is that the KG itself is known to be near when the signs of the end of the age happen, as the summer is known to be near when all the trees sprout leaves.

Look at the fig tree and all the trees. When they sprout leaves, you can see for yourselves and know that summer is near. Even so, when you see these things happening, you know that the kingdom of God is near. (Luke 21:29–33)

The fifteen KG production functions are to be summarized as follows.

The production outputs are the crop, wheat, big tree, big dough, treasure, fine pearls, good fish, new and old treasures, forgiven account, hiring and paying, wedding banquet, oil, double talents, grain, and KG itself, which indicate the outputs of the WG.

The raw materials are the seed, good seed, mustard seed, yeast, treasure, fine pearls, good fish, new and old treasures, debts, hiring and paying, wedding clothes, oil, talents, seed, and signs of the end of the age, which show the inputs of the WG.

The labor inputs are to scatter, sow and gather, collect, throw, and scatter, as we live his ruling by submitting to and participating in laboring.

The capital inputs are to plant, mix, buy, bring out, forgive, agree, wear, take, work, and happen, as we live his ruling by submitting to and participating in being invested into spiritually.

God rules the KG with the outputs of the WG like the production outputs of the KG production functions as shown above. We as the people of the KG live God's kingdom with the outputs of the WG by submitting to and participating in the spiritual labors and spiritual investments.

THEMES/ATTRIBUTES/CHARACTERISTICS OF THE OUTPUTS OF THE WORD OF GOD

JC taught the KG, which God rules over with the outputs of the word of God, in utilizing parables indicating the KG production functions. What are the outputs of the WG? The outputs of the word of God in the Bible are revealed as three themes/attributes/characteristics, namely, the holiness, love, and glory of God. The four Gospels explain how to rule the thematic rules by God and how to live our thematic lives according to and with the outputs of

The Kingdom of God in the Bible: The Glorious Biblical Life

the word of God, which are the themes/attributes/characteristics of God, namely, the holiness, love, and glory of God.

LIFE FOR THE HOLINESS OF GOD

God rules the KG with holiness, with which the children of God should live the life by submitting to and participating in. The Bible teaches us the attitudes, positive actions, and negative actions of living life for the holiness of God.

Three attitudes for the holiness of God are:

First Attitude for the Holiness of God

The first attitude is to believe the way of righteousness.

> For John came to you to show you the way of righteousness, and you did not believe him, but the tax collectors and the prostitutes did. And even after you saw this, you did not repent and believe him. (Matt 21:32)

Second Attitude for the Holiness of God

The second attitude is to repent of sin.

> Repent, for the kingdom of heaven is near. (Matt 4:17)

Third Attitude of the Holiness of God

The third attitude is to be poor in the Spirit, to be humble, and to be born again.

> Blessed are the poor in spirit, for theirs is the kingdom of heaven. (Matt 5:3)
>
> Therefore, whoever humbles himself like this child is the greatest in the kingdom of heaven. (Matt 18:4)

> I tell you the truth, no one can see the kingdom of God unless he is born again. (John 3:3).

Three positive participations for the holiness of God are:

First Positive Participation for the Holiness of God

The first positive participation is to seek first righteousness.

> But seek first his kingdom and his righteousness, and all these things will be given to you as well. (Matt 6:33)

Second Positive Participation for the Holiness of God

The second positive participation is to hear and understand, to practice and teach, to preach, to pray, to do, to know, to produce, and to receive the message, the commandments, the message, the will, the message, the secrets, the fruits, and the keys of the KG.

> When anyone hears the message about the kingdom and does not understand it, the evil one comes and snatches away what was sown in his heart. This is the seed sown in his heart. (Matt 13:19)

> Anyone who breaks one of the least of these commandments and teaches others to do the same will be called least in the kingdom of heaven, but whoever practices and teaches these commands will be called great in the kingdom of heaven. (Matt 5:19)

> As you go, preach this message: "The kingdom of heaven has come near." (Matt 10:7)

> Your kingdom come, your will be done on earth as it is in heaven. (Matt 6:10)

> Not everyone who says to me, Lord, Lord, will enter the kingdom of heaven, but only he does the will of my Father who is in heaven. (Matt 7:21)

> The knowledge of the secrets of the kingdom of heaven has been given to you, but not to them. (Matt 13:11)

The Kingdom of God in the Bible: The Glorious Biblical Life

> Therefore I tell you that the kingdom of heaven will be taken away from you and given a people who will produce its fruit. (Matt 21:43)

> I will give you the keys of the kingdom of heaven; whatever you bind on earth will be bound in heaven, and whatever you loose on earth will be loosed in heaven. (Matt 16:19)

Third Positive Participation for the Holiness of God

The third positive participation is to see the kingdom of God coming with power and forcefully advancing.

> I tell you the truth, some who are standing here will not taste death before they see the kingdom of God come with power. (Mark 9:1)

> From the days of John the Baptist until now, the kingdom of heaven has been forcefully advancing, and forceful men lay hold of it. (Matt 11:12).

Three negative participation for the holiness of God are:

First Negative Participation for the Holiness of God

The first negative participation is not to be rich, not to look back, to assert the KG not of this world, to wipe off dust, and to drive out demons.

> I tell you the truth, it is hard for a rich man to enter the kingdom of heaven. (Matt 19:23)

> No one who puts his hand to the plow and looks back is fit for service in the kingdom of God. (Luke 9:62)

> My kingdom is not of this world. If it were, my servants would fight to prevent my arrest by the Jewish leaders. But now my kingdom is from another place. (John 18:36)

> Even the dust of your town that sticks to our feet we wipe off against you. Yet be sure of this: The kingdom of God is near. (Luke 10:11)

> But if I drive out demons by the finger of God, then the kingdom of God has come to you. (Luke 11:20)

Second Negative Participation for the Holiness of God

The second negative participation is to do the righteousness surpassing that of the Pharisees and the teachers of the law and not to be hypocrites.

> For I tell you that unless your righteousness surpasses that of the Pharisees and the teachers of the law, you will certainly not enter the kingdom of heaven. (Matt 5:20)

> Woe to you, teachers of the law and Pharisees, you hypocrites! You shut the kingdom of heaven in men's faces. You yourselves do not enter, nor will you let those enter who are trying to. (Matt 23:13)

Third Negative Participation for the Holiness of God

The third negative participation is to be persecuted because of righteousness.

> Blessed are those who are persecuted because of righteousness, for theirs is the kingdom of heaven. (Matt 5:10)

LIFE FOR THE LOVE OF GOD

God rules the kingdom with his love and grace, while the children of God should live the life by submitting to and participating in them.

Two positive participations for the love of God are:

First Positive Participation for the Love of God

The first positive participation is to accept the kingdom of God with pleasure by selling possessions and giving to the poor.

> Do not be afraid, little flock, for your Father has been pleased to give you the kingdom. Sell your possessions and give to the poor. (Luke 12:32–33)

Second Positive Participation for the Love of God

The second positive participation is to love your God and your neighbor and to heal the sick.

> The most important one is this: Hear, O Israel, the Lord our God, the Lord is one. Love the Lord your God with all your heart and with all your soul and with all your mind and with all your strength. The second is this: Love your neighbor as yourself. There is no commandment greater than these. (Mark 12:29–31)

> Heal the sick who are there and tell them, The kingdom of God is near you. (Luke 10:9)

LIFE FOR THE GLORY OF GOD

God rules the kingdom for his glory, while the children of God should live the life by participating in it and revealing it. Two positive participations revealing the glory of God are:

First Positive Participation for the Glory of God

The first positive participation is to see all the prophets and to take places in the feast in the kingdom of God, which JC prepares.

> There will be weeping there, and gnashing of teeth, when you see Abraham, Isaac and Jacob and all the prophets in the kingdom of God, but you yourselves thrown out.

People will come from east and west and north and south, and will take their places at the feast in the kingdom of God. (Luke 13:28-29)

In my Father's house are many rooms; if it were not so, I would have told you. I am going there to prepare a place for you. (John 14:2)

Second Positive Participation for the Glory of God

The second positive participation is to eat and drink at JC's table and to sit on thrones, judging the twelve tribes of Israel.

So that you may eat and drink at my table in my kingdom and sit on thrones, judging the twelve tribes of Israel. (Luke 22:30)

In summary, JC taught the kingdom of God in seventy-three verses of the four Gospels, which include seventeen parables and fifty-six expositions.

The seventeen parables indicate the fifteen kingdom-of-God production functions, which produce the outputs of the word of God by the inputs of the seeds, labor, and capital of the word of God.

The fifty-six expositions of the kingdom of God emphasize the themes, attributes, and characteristics of God in the kingdom of God, which are the holiness, love, and glory of God. God rules the kingdom of God with three themes, and then the children of God should live the life by submitting to and participating in three themes.

JC taught on the kingdom of God:

Life for the holiness of God—three attitudes, three positive participations, three negative participations

Life for the love of God—two positive participations

Life for the glory of God—two positive participations

CHAPTER 15

Conclusion

THE ULTIMATE PURPOSE OF the Christian faith is to live life in the kingdom of God. There are two aspects of the KG revealed in the Bible. The future aspect of the KG is the perfect KG illustrated in the garden of Eden, in the second coming of Jesus Christ, and in the new heaven and new earth shown in Revelation. The present aspect of the KG is the KG coming near as said by Jesus Christ beginning to preach. What is the present aspect of the KG, and what is life in the present aspect of the KG? Our life in the present aspect of the KG should be ruled by God, and the rule by God could be understood as the characteristics (attributes) of God that are recognized. God's characteristics can be classified into the natural characteristics and the active (moral) characteristics: the natural characteristics are spiritual, changeless, all powerful, all knowing, everywhere, and eternal; the active (moral) characteristics are glorious, holy, righteous, gracious and loving, truthful, and wise.

The life ruled by God in terms of his natural characters is defined as the spiritual life (SL) lived in Jesus Christ, and the life ruled by God in terms of his active characteristics is the glorious life (GL) controlled by Jesus Christ who stays in me. The spiritual life is to live as God's people, as Jesus Christ's pupils, and as Spirit-filled persons. And the glorious life includes the glorious economic life and the glorious biblical life. The glorious economic life indicates the GL applying the economic theories, and the glorious biblical life is the GL illustrated by Jesus Christ using the parables in the Bible.

In summary, life in the present aspect of the KG includes three areas of life: (1) the spiritual life, (2) the glorious economic life, and (3) the glorious biblical life.

The spiritual life is:

1. Spiritual life
    1. As God's people
    2. As Jesus Christ's pupils
    3. As Spirit-filled persons

The glorious economic lives are:

2. Identity of economic man and woman
    1. Self-interest with stewardship
    2. Rationality with holiness
3. Decision-making
    1. Relative private property rights
4. Trade (exchange)
    1. Division of labor
    2. Competition
    3. Public sector
5. National economy
    1. Gross Domestic Product
    2. Inflation (money)
    3. Employment
6. Production by labor
    1. Population
    2. Labor
    3. Employment
7. Production by capital
    1. Saving
    2. Investment management
    3. Investment for technology
    4. Investment sources
8. Production optimization
    1. Production factors optimization
    2. Production output optimization

Conclusion

9. Consumption by freedom
   1. Consumption for utility
10. Consumption by temptation
    1. Consumerism
    2. Consumption of evil as good
11. Family economy
    1. Fundamental biblical truths
    2. Living biblical truths
    3. Christian biblical truths
12. Social welfare functions
    1. Libertarianism
    2. Liberalism
    3. Utilitarianism
13. Economic policies
    1. Market failures
    2. Business fluctuations

The glorious biblical life is:

14. Glorious biblical life
    1. Kingdom-of-God production functions
    2. Thematic (holy; gracious and loving; glorious) lives

In conclusion, the life for faith in the present aspect of the KG is:

1. To live in seeking the KG and his righteousness above all as God's people; in following Jesus Christ, burdened with the cross given to them as Jesus Christ's pupils; and in living with the vision, gifts, and fruits of the Spirit, as Spirit-filled persons, implied in the spiritual life (ch 1)
2. To live by implementing the biblical truths concerning economic identity, economic principles, production, consumption, distribution, and policies, implied in the glorious economic life (chs. 2–13)
3. To live the KG production functions of the word of God indicated in the parables on the KG and themes of the holiness-love-glory implied in the glorious biblical life (ch. 14)

Bibliography

Arrow, Kenneth. *Social Choice and Individual Values*. New York: Wiley, 1951.

Baumrind, Diana. "Child Care Practices Anteceding Three Patterns of Preschool Behavior." *Genetic Psychology Monographs* 75 (1967) 43–88.

Bentham, Jeremy. *An Introduction to the Principles of Morals and Legislation*. Oxford, UK: Clarendon, 1907.

Condorcet, Marquis de. "Essay on the Application of Analysis to the Probability of Majority Decisions." 1785. Further information unavailable.

Economist. "Economic Data, Commodities and Markets." *Economist*, July 17, 2021. https://www.economist.com/economic-and-financial-indicators/2021/07/17/economic-data-commodities-and-markets.

Edgeworth, Francis Ysidro. *Mathematical Psychics: An Essay on the Application of Mathematics to the Moral Sciences*. London: Paul and Co., 1881. https://onlinebooks.library.upenn.edu/webbin/book/lookupid?key=olbp34052.

Fayol, Henri. *Administration industrielle et générale*. Paris: Dunod, 1941.

Keynes, John Maynard. *The General Theory of Employment, Interest, and Money*. London: Macmillan, 1936.

Lockyer, Herbert, Sr., ed. *Nelson's Illustrated Bible Dictionary*. Nashville: Nelson, 1986.

Mankiw, N. Gregory. *Principles of Economics*. 9th ed. San Diego, CA: Harcourt College, 2020.

Marx, Karl. *Das Kapital*. N.p.: Meisner, 1983.

Mill, John Stuart. *Utilitarianism*. London: Fraser, 1861.

Nobel Prize. "Press Release: The Prize in Economic Sciences 2019." Nobel Prize, Oct. 14, 2019. https://www.nobelprize.org/prizes/economic-sciences/2019/press-release/.

Nozick, Robert. *Anarchy, State, and Utopia*. Oxford, UK: Blackwell, 1974.

Pareto, Vilfredo. *Manual di economia Politica* [Manual of Political Economy]. Milano, It.: Societa Editrice, 1906.

Peterson, Peter G. *Gray Dawn: How the Coming Age Wave Will Transform America—and the World*. New York: Times, 1999.

Piketty, Thomas. *Capital in the Twenty-First Century*. Translated by Arthur Goldhammer. Cambridge, MA: Belknap, 2014.

Bibliography

Pindyck, Robert S., and Daniel L. Rubinfeld. *Microeconomics.* 9th ed. Upper Saddle River, NJ: Pearson, 2021.
Rawls, John. *A Theory of Justice.* Cambridge, MA: Belknap, 1971.
Schumpeter, Joseph A. *Capitalism, Socialism, and Democracy.* New York: Harper, 1942.
Smith, Adam. *An Inquiry into the Nature and Causes of the Wealth of Nations.* London: Strahan and Cadell, 1779.
Twitchell, James B. *Lead Us into Temptation: The Triumph of American Materialism.* New York: Columbia University Press, 1999.

ONLINE RESOURCES

Pew Research Center (www.pewresearch.org)
Transparency International (www.transparency.org)
United States Bureau of Economic Analysis (www.bea.gov)
United States Bureau of Labor Statistics (www.bls.gov)
United States Census Bureau (www.census.gov)
United States Central Intelligence Agency (www.cia.gov)
United States Civil Rights Act 1964 (https://www.dol.gov/agencies/oasam/civil-rights-center/statutes/civil-rights-act-of-1964)
United States Federal Reserve (www.federalreserve.gov)
World Bank (www.worldbank.org)

www.ingramcontent.com/pod-product-compliance
Lightning Source LLC
Chambersburg PA
CBHW071152090426
42736CB00012B/2302